# UNDERSTANDING APPRENTICESHIPS

## *A Student's Guide*

**BEN ROWLAND**

trotman t

*Understanding Apprenticeships*

First edition published in 2023 by Trotman, an imprint of Trotman Indigo Publishing, 21d Charles Street, Bath, BA1 1HX

© Trotman Indigo Publishing Ltd 2023

**Author**: Ben Rowland

**British Library Cataloguing in Publication Data**
A catalogue record for this book is available from the British Library

ISBN: 978 1 912943 95 1

Printed and bound by Ashford Colour Press Ltd

All details in this book were correct at the time of going to press, but there are new and exciting developments happening in the world of apprenticeships all the time. To keep up to date with all the latest news and updates use this QR code or visit **indigo.careers/ understanding_apprenticeships**.

# Contents

About the author      vi

Acknowledgements      vi

Endorsements      viii

**1   Introduction**      **1**

1.1   The 21st century is the apprenticeship century      3

1.2   A bit more on this guidebook and how to use it      9

Summary      14

Apprentice Case Study: Janelle Raphanahane      15

Employer Case Study: Arc Group London      16

**2   The power of apprenticeships**      **19**

Introduction      20

2.1   Why apprenticeships work      21

2.2   Almost all careers are now accessible through an apprenticeship      24

2.3   Employers see the value of apprenticeships      27

2.4   Young people see the value of apprenticeships      32

2.5   Governments see the value of apprenticeships      37

2.6   Schools and colleges see the value of apprenticeships      41

Summary      43

Apprentice Case Study: Olly Newman      44

Employer Case Study: Henry Boot      45

**3   What an apprenticeship entails**      **47**

Introduction      48

3.1   An apprenticeship is a job      49

3.2   What an apprenticeship programme is      51

3.3   How an apprenticeship works      53

3.4   How you pass an apprenticeship and become qualified      55

3.5   What are all the different apprenticeship 'levels'?      57

3.6   English and maths, aka functional skills      61

3.7   Who are all the different organisations involved?      63

3.8   Who pays for your apprenticeship and what are the financial implications?      65

3.9   Things to watch out for      68

Summary      73

Apprentice Case Study: Chris Smith      75

Employer Case Study: BT Group      76

**4    What you need to know about university
and other options                                79**

Introduction                                                      80
4.1   The reasons to go to university                             82
4.2   The reasons to think twice about going to university        85
4.3   Understanding pro-university bias                           90
4.4   How to handle pro-university bias                           95
4.5   Other options                                               96
Summary                                                           100
Apprentice Case Study: Lili Wilson                                102
Employer Case Study: The NHS                                      103

**5    Deciding whether to do an apprenticeship    105**

Introduction                                                      106
5.1   Why this decision is not forever                            107
5.2   Is now a good time for you to embark on an apprenticeship?  109
5.3   What attributes do you need to succeed in an apprenticeship?  114
5.4   What kind of apprenticeship might be right for me?          119
Summary                                                           130
Apprentice Case Study: Sophie Mawson                             131
Employer Case Study: Troup Bywaters + Anders                     132

**6    Finding a good apprenticeship to apply for    135**

Introduction                                                      136
6.1   Geography: which employers can you physically get to?       137
6.2   What apprenticeships should you consider?                   139
6.3   How to find apprenticeships to apply for                    152
6.4   How to evaluate employers and training providers            160
Summary                                                           164
Apprentice Case Study: Tom Ballard                                165
Employer Case Study: McDonald's                                   166

**7 Getting a great apprenticeship** **167**

Introduction 168

7.1 Know your 'story' for each apprenticeship 170

7.2 Navigating the application process 174

7.3 Assessing the apprenticeship 181

7.4 Responding appropriately 184

Summary 185

Apprentice Case Study: Jack Bonfield 186

Employer Case Study: Network Rail 187

**8 Apprenticeships are for everyone** **189**

Introduction 190

8.1 People from a minority ethnic background 191

8.2 People with special educational needs, disabilities and
    other additional needs 193

8.3 People who are care-experienced 198

8.4 People who are not in employment, education or training (NEET) 199

Summary 201

Apprentice Case Study: George Eiloart 202

Employer Case Study: IBM 203

**9 Conclusion** **205**

Apprentice Case Study: Michaela Clack 207

Employer Case Study: MBDA 208

**10 Useful resources** **211**

# About the author

Ben Rowland is a leading expert and advisor on apprenticeships and post-school options.

Ben founded the pioneering apprenticeships programme Arch Apprentices in 2012. Spurred on by a desire to bring world-class educational standards to apprenticeships, this unique training provider created groundbreaking new apprenticeships in occupations such as digital marketing and advertising. Arch was a recognised innovator in apprenticeship programme delivery, and persuaded companies such as Google and Facebook to embrace apprenticeships for the first time. Ben also worked with hundreds of small businesses, government departments, NHS Trusts and charities as Arch grew to be the eighth biggest provider of apprenticeships in the UK, supporting tens of thousands of young people to take their first steps in their new careers. Ben also served for five years on the government's Apprenticeship Stakeholder Board, advising on apprenticeship implementation.

Since 2019, when Ben helped Arch Apprentices to merge with fellow learning provider, Avado Learning, he has been working as an independent consultant, advising a range of organisations on their careers, development, learning and change programmes.

Prior to starting Arch Apprentices, Ben founded RSe Consulting, a boutique consultancy firm subsequently acquired by Tribal Group plc, and was Chair of Toynbee Hall, the social action charity, for six years.

Ben is a passionate advocate for vocational education and what it can offer to individuals, employers and society. He holds two university degrees and understands the value of higher education. He is committed to providing young people – and their families – with the objective information and insight they need to navigate their post-school options.

# Acknowledgements

This book encapsulates the experiences, insights and ideas of many people. I feel less like an original author and more like a spokesperson for everyone who believes that young people deserve to have the wherewithal to figure out whether an apprenticeship could be right for them. I would like to say thank you, however, to a few organisations and people in particular.

Jason Holt for encouraging me to persist with the book, ably backed by Jane Rowland (my mother) – although Jason and Jane have never met, I know they would approve of each other and their respective efforts to keep me to task.

My former colleagues from Arch, who have provided encouragement and insight, in particular Anita Ibrahim for her input on challenges for young people from a minority ethnic background.

Neurodiversity In Business and Digital Advantage, who have advised me on the challenges for people who are neurodivergent.

Anthony Impey from Be The Business for his input around small and medium businesses.

The Association of Colleges and the Association of Employment & Learning Providers (AELP), who have encouraged and supported the book from the start.

The Association of Apprentices, who brought together such a helpful and insightful focus group of apprentices to feed into the book.

All the employers who are case studies in the book, and the many dozens of others with whom I have worked over the last decade.

All the apprentices who are case studies, both those that are in the book and those who are part of the bonus downloadable material, and the many hundreds of amazing young people I have worked with over the last decade – you are all an inspiration.

My own teenage children, who are coming up to decisions about what they do next – you are the extra motivation, as well as being very cool kids.

Finally, Marie, who has inspired, energised and made me believe (in many ways) from the moment I first told her about the book (the day we met) all the way until now.

# Endorsements

**"** *Understanding Apprenticeships* is comprehensive, authoritative and engaging – a must-read for anyone exploring their post-school options.

*Lindsay Conroy, UCAS Apprenticeship National Programme Lead*

**"** An essential and informative guide - if you want to know about apprenticeships, figure out how apprenticeships compare with other options or to help you go about finding and succeeding in an apprenticeship then this is a book for you.

*Simon Ashworth, Director of Policy, Association of Employment and Learning Providers*

**"** A must-read for anyone thinking about their next steps or supporting those doing so. It brings together various perspectives of apprentice-ships, crammed with insight and knowledge, as well as being full of practical tips and tools.

*Daniel Lally, Director of Business Engagement, Skills and Employability, Sheffield Hallam University*

**"** *Understanding Apprenticeships* brings great insight for anyone considering whether an apprenticeship is for them. What it is, how it works, what it feels like to do one all jump off the page. A great resource for young people, adults, parents, advisers and employers.

*David Hughes CBE, Chief Executive, Association of Colleges*

**"** A must-read for any young person considering their options for their post-school career. Apprenticeships are increasingly viewed by employers as a vital recruitment route, and this book helps explain what they are, how they work and how to figure out whether they are right for you. Frank, engaging and authoritative, I highly recommend it.

*Anthony Impey, Chief Executive, Be the Business*

**"** At long last, thanks to the brilliant Ben Rowland, we have a why, what, and how guide on apprenticeships. Still a necessity in light of the difficulties in sourcing the right information, this book is a must read for would be apprentices, their parents and teachers. It dispels the myths, signposts where to find further information and enthuses the reader about why they might want to join the apprenticeship revolution.

*Jason Holt CBE, CEO & Founder, Metaverse Learning*

# Section 1
# Introduction

# Welcome – and congratulations!

What for?

Well, for considering that an apprenticeship could be the right way for you to start your career. And you are correct – it could be a *brilliant* way for you to start a new career, perhaps even the best way. And many hundreds of thousands of other people just like you – both here in the UK and around the world – and their families and teachers, are beginning to think this too.

But it can be quite a hard decision to make, as there are lots of people who might advise you to go down another route, and they can seem so sure of themselves.

It is hard to find balanced, unbiased information about what apprenticeships are really like – 'warts and all' – and how to go about getting one. It is also hard to know which apprenticeship might be right for you.

And finally, applying for apprenticeships is also complicated – certainly a bit more complicated than applying for a place at university or a regular job.

So, this book is for you, and for people advising you.

It's here to:

- give you the full picture on apprenticeships
- help you figure out how they compare to other options and whether they are right for you
- show you how to find and succeed in an apprenticeship, should you choose that route.

*A quick note: while 90% of the book applies to anyone anywhere in the UK considering doing an apprenticeship, the description of the Government apprenticeship scheme is of the English scheme only. Notes on where the content applies to England specifically are included in chapters 3.4, 3.6, 3.7, 3.8, 4.2 and 6.2.*

# 1.1 The 21st century is the apprenticeship century

Why is it such a sensible option to consider an apprenticeship as the next step in your journey?

There are five main reasons to be excited about apprenticeships in the 21st century.

1. More and more employers, in all sectors and of all shapes and sizes, now love apprenticeships.
2. You can get into almost any career through an apprenticeship.
3. Governments around the world want and need apprenticeships, including here in the UK.
4. Apprenticeships might be your best route to maximising the money in your pocket.
5. Apprenticeships are driven by the economics of the 21st century.

## 1. The employers offering apprenticeships

More and more of the UK's best employers, from Jaguar Land Rover to BAE Systems to Sainsburys to IBM, are increasing the number of apprenticeships they offer – and, in some cases, quite dramatically. The 'Big 4' accountancy firms (Deloitte, PwC, KPMG and EY), long seen as the 'gold standard' for graduate recruitment, now recruit as many apprentices as they do individuals through their graduate schemes.

And where the big and well-known companies lead, other companies typically follow. Apprenticeships are now increasingly seen as a 'high end' option and carry more recognition and prestige than they ever have. This change has largely occurred over the last ten years, and has been significant; and it will continue to grow as those people now at the start of their careers who have done apprenticeships start to make their (rapid) way up the career ladder. I see this with those who were apprentices back in 2013 and 2014, who are now emerging as leaders in their businesses and promoting apprenticeships like mad.

You will see throughout this book case studies from different employers, from the biggest ones you have definitely heard of – such as BT and the NHS – and those you almost certainly have not.

You can read a bit more on why employers are coming to love apprenticeships more and more in Chapter 2.3.

## 2. The careers you can access via an apprenticeship

There is now almost no career you cannot access through an apprenticeship. There are over 600 different apprenticeship standards that you can do, from traditional 'trades' (such as plumbers, electricians and carpenters) to advanced engineering to digital and IT to medical, health and care (as of 2024 you can become a fully qualified doctor entirely through an apprenticeship) to creative industries to public sector to professional services… the list goes on and on.

There are apprenticeships at many different levels, from Level 2 all the way up to Level 7, so there is something for everyone (you can find out more information on these levels in chapter 3.5).

An apprenticeship is increasingly seen as ambitious and impressive qualification – though you may have to convince a few people along the way.

A growing number of apprenticeships (Levels 6 and 7) are now 'degree apprenticeships', meaning you can get a degree (exactly as you would get from university) while earning money and getting valuable work experience in a real job – at the same time.

Throughout this book you will find case studies of real people who have done a variety of apprenticeships, and in Chapter 6.2 you can read a bit more about the different kinds of apprenticeships available.

## 3. Governments want & need apprenticeships

Apprenticeships are taking off all around the world.

Some of the world's strongest economies have had apprenticeships baked into how they develop skills for decades, such as Germany, Austria and Switzerland. Many other countries are only now realising just what apprenticeships can do for their economies: from Australia to America, from India to Indonesia, from South Africa to Sweden, governments are developing apprenticeship programmes as a key way to develop their economies.

There is a reason why this is the case: as economies around the world develop and change, one thing that is common to many of them is that they cannot find enough workers with the skills they need.

While governments continue to support university level education, they are increasingly concerned that university education alone is not going to provide the skilled people their economies need. As many of the employers in the case studies in this book show, university graduates do not always have the knowledge, skills and approaches that employers are looking for. And governments are listening to what employers are saying about this and investing in apprenticeship programmes as a result.

In the UK, the Government continues to invest huge amounts of time and effort in promoting apprenticeships. Every major political party in the UK supports them – so even if the Government changes through a general election, apprenticeships are not going anywhere.

You can read more about what different governments around the world are doing in Chapter 2.5, including the UK Government (and what a possible future government might do).

## 4. Earning power

A 2016 report, *Productivity and Lifetime Earnings of Apprentices and Graduates*, by the Centre for Economics and Business Research (CEBR) on behalf of Barclays Bank, found that people getting a Level 4 apprenticeship earned as much over their lifetime as the typical graduate. Since then, the quality of apprenticeships has grown, which is likely to have improved earning prospects even further.

Two other factors need to be considered when it comes to the money:

i.   If you do an apprenticeship you start your earning journey three years earlier than if you go to university; you also get three extra years of progressing up the career ladder, promotions and pay rises. It is common for someone who has done an apprenticeship that when they are three years into their career (i.e. the age they would have been leaving university if they had chosen to study for a degree instead) to be earning comfortably more than someone just starting out as a graduate from university; and they are already on a steep upward career trajectory towards more promotions and pay rises.

ii. Doing an apprenticeship avoids the costs and subsequent debt involved with going to university – you have nothing to pay back once you have finished – a saving of thousands of pounds.

## 5. Apprenticeships & 21st-century economics

Apprenticeships are here to stay, not just because employers like them at the moment or because they are popular with governments right now. They are here to stay because they are the best logical response to the needs of the 21st-century global economy.

That's because the 21st-century economy is beginning to look very different from the 20th-century economy – it is beginning to look like an Apprenticeship Economy: one in which rapidly changing skills requirements call for shorter, more nimble, hands-on practical training and education, and employees who are fully adapted to this way of acquiring productivity for their employers.

There are a number of reasons why the economy is changing so quickly.

*First*, the pace of technology-driven change has never been as fast – and it's getting faster. Technological change is not new and has been disrupting how we live for centuries: the arrival of the printing press in the 15th century changed everything back then, and the invention of the steam engine was the spark for the UK's industrial revolution of the 18th and 19th centuries.

But technological change has never moved more quickly than now. We can see this by comparing how long it took key technology breakthroughs to reach 100 million users.

- Colour TV: launched in the mid-1950s, took **25 years** to reach 100 million users.
- Microsoft Windows: launched in the mid-1980s, took **15 years** to reach the 100 million mark.
- Spotify: launched in 2006, took **four years** to reach the same number.
- Instagram: launched in 2010, took **two years** to reach that milestone.

- TikTok: launched in 2016, took **nine months**.
- ChatGPT: launched in early 2023, took just **two months** to reach 100 million users.

*Second*, not much is certain any more. Politics is as unpredictable as it has been for a long time. That's true here in the UK (where we have had as many Prime Ministers since 2016 as we had in the 36 years between 1979 and 2015!) and also in other countries. China and Russia are not on the paths to Western democracy that we thought they were. This political uncertainty means we can no longer rely on assumptions about how the world will be in five years' time, let alone 20 years.

*Third*, the physical world we live in is under pressure like never before: while scientists and (most) politicians agree that climate change is happening, we don't know exactly how it will change things. We recently learned that a new virus can literally shut the world down – and who knows if and when the next one will be on the way?

*Fourth*, more optimistically, there are potentially huge positive breakthroughs on the way that will change our lives forever. For example, nuclear fusion (which would enable almost free, limitless energy) is getting closer – maybe; and new materials technology with new substances such as graphene and lignin could change what we can create and how, for the better.

*Fifth*, the world of work itself is changing. Employee expectations are changing fast: gone are the days of dutifully turning up to work every day at 9am and doing whatever your boss told you until it was time to clock off at 5pm. Employees now expect that their work will be meaningful and enjoyable, with opportunities to influence management, and are also looking for a flexible approach when it comes to the hours and the location of their work.

All of these huge changes and uncertainties mean that jobs are changing fast. This, in turn, means employers are constantly having to update the jobs they employ people for. But they face a huge battle in finding people with the necessary skills for these new jobs – because the skills are so new, very few people have them. So they now realise that to cope with the 21st-century economy they have to 'grow their own' and develop people to learn the skills they need; they cannot rely on others – like schools and universities – to do this for them.

**Twenty-first-century employers want to hire people who may not yet have the skills they need, but who are willing and able to learn them. They want employees who are action-orientated and who like getting things done. They want to take these people – the raw material – and train and shape them.**

This is, in fact, a description of exactly what apprenticeships do. And that is why apprenticeships are made for the 21st century.

This is amazing news for anyone who comes from a 'non-traditional' background or who has a disability or health issue. Twenty years ago, and maybe even ten years ago, to get a job in any organisation it definitely helped if you 'looked' and 'behaved' in the same way as the people who already worked there; but the shortage of skills around the world is making companies challenge their biases head-on, in order that they can hire the skilled people they need, regardless of what they look or sound like.

So that's why I started by saying 'Well done', because considering an apprenticeship is a very smart thing to do if you want to set yourself up for a successful career in the 21st century.

# 1.2 A bit more on this guidebook and how to use it

The purpose of this book is to give you information on and insights about apprenticeships as an option for starting your career in a way that means you feel you can make a decision you are happy with.

There is, of course, tons of information out there on the internet. Search 'Should I do an apprenticeship?' on Google, TikTok or any other platform and you will get thousands of results. However, quantity doesn't always mean quality. The information you find typically falls into one of three categories.

i.   Worthy but dull technical content often produced by the government or other 'official' organisations. It may be accurate, but is unlikely to address the real questions you may have or do so in a way that you actually want to read.

ii.  Promotion of apprenticeships as the best thing since sliced bread. Normally this is from organisations that stand to gain from more people taking up apprenticeships; this information is typically more engaging and inspiring, but is often not objective, and may skim over the downsides that you need to know about.

iii. Inspirational case studies and testimonials from 'superstar' award-winning apprentices. These stories can really bring apprenticeships alive and are directly from people like you, but by definition they are not typical stories. They rarely explain the nuts and bolts of how an apprenticeship works, or answer the question of 'How can this work for me?'.

It is hard to find structured, independent but also engaging advice and guidance that makes sense. Therefore, the intention of this book is threefold.

i.   To give you enough insight and knowledge, combined with some tips, tools and techniques, for you to be able to figure out with a reasonable degree of confidence whether an apprenticeship is right for you.

ii. If you do decide that an apprenticeship is the right route for you, to help you figure out which ones to go for and how to best go about getting the one you want.

iii. To equip you with talking points so that you can have even more productive conversations with those advising you: friends, parents, teachers and careers advisors.

It is absolutely NOT a book designed to 'persuade' you to do an apprenticeship.

There are good reasons for doing an apprenticeship; and there are reasons to be cautious about doing an apprenticeship. There are good reasons for pursuing other options, like uni or a year out; and, likewise, there are reasons to be cautious about them as well. This book looks at all of the options as objectively as possible.

You may want to know what qualifies me to write this book. There are four things that are probably relevant.

i. I have made many different choices around my career: I took a year out after school to travel and see the world (well, Africa at least); I went to university (two of them in fact); I have been on dozens of corporate training programmes, from the terrible to the life-changing; and more recently I trained and qualified in a totally new vocational career (as a personal trainer).

ii. I set up and ran an apprenticeship programme that worked with employers large and small, famous (Google, Barclays Bank, John Lewis & Partners) and not-so-famous. This programme evolved into one of the biggest apprenticeship programmes in the UK. This means I have seen with my own eyes how apprenticeships (really) work – and what happens when they go wrong. I have also undertaken lots of further research on apprenticeships while writing this book.

iii. I have employed apprentices and seen first-hand what they can do, and what enables an apprentice to succeed.

iv. I have two teenage children myself (at the time of writing), who are 13 and 16. The advice and information in this book are the advice and information I give to them.

This guidebook has ten sections that take you through the key aspects of apprenticeships.

Section 1.    **Introduction**: Welcome to the apprenticeship century.

Section 2.    **The Power of Apprenticeships**: how they deliver value and why lots of different people are seeing their value more and more.

Section 3.    **What an apprenticeship entails**: the components, End Point Assessment, different levels, functional skills, who's involved, financial implications, things to beware of.

Section 4.    **What you need to know about university and other options**: the benefits of university, things to think about, managing pro-university bias.

Section 5.    **Deciding whether to do an apprenticeship**: your timing and circumstances, your attributes, evaluating apprenticeships for you (your aspirations, strengths, etc.).

Section 6.    **Finding a good apprenticeship to apply for**: location, which apprenticeships (occupation, sector, type of employer), managing your applications, finding apprenticeships online and offline, evaluating employers and providers.

Section 7.    **Getting a great apprenticeship**: establishing your story, navigating the application process, assessing the offer, responding appropriately.

Section 8.    **Apprenticeships are for everyone**: additional advice for people with extra (perceived) challenges (minority ethnic community, disability, neurodivergence, mental health issues, NEET, those who are care-experienced).

Section 9.    **Conclusion**

Section 10.  **Useful resources**: a list of organisations and sources of information that can be helpful to you.

Between each section there are two case studies, one from an apprentice and one from an employer. The **Apprentice Case Studies** are from people who completed their apprenticeship up to ten years ago, so you can see what they have gone on to do. I have focused these case studies on 'normal' apprentices – not award winners or 'superstars' – because it is the more normal experiences that are likely to be more relevant to you. There are also five bonus apprentice case studies available online at indigo.careers.

Throughout this book there are **Interesting ideas** – things for you to consider, and which may add to your decision-making process.

This book is here to help you make the right decision for yourself. Not by persuading you or even showing you, but by giving you the structure and questions to come to the right conclusion for you, whether that is doing an apprenticeship now, later or not at all.

You should use this book in whatever way helps you most. Here is one suggested way to use this book.

- Have a look at the chapter headings to see what is covered and how it flows
- Allow yourself a sneak preview of those chapters that you are most interested in
- Then read the whole book through, quite quickly – though don't worry about skipping the chapters that don't grab your attention (you can always come back to them)
- Re-read those chapters that you find most useful and interesting
- Download the tools that are available online at **indigo. careers/understanding_apprenticeships** and start to use them
- Then keep the book on your desk or by your bed so you can dip back into it whenever you want.

I've kept the chapters deliberately short, so if you only have a few spare minutes you can still read a chunk of something useful.

# 💡 Interesting idea: Unhelpful helpful people

There are likely to be lots of people who will have an opinion on what you should do after you leave education, and – because 99% of human beings are quite nice – they probably want to help you: they want to be helpful. This might include your teachers, your parents, relatives or a family friend.

But however helpful they want to be, they will not necessarily know much about the things that matter right now for your choices: about the jobs market, about careers, about modern employers, or even that much about you and what your real strengths and preferences are.

They may well be looking at your choices as though they were 'their' choices when they were your age and reliving them (especially if they regret their choices, or perhaps that they did not have the choices you have).

So while they may be well-meaning, it is also possible that they may be unintentionally *unhelpful*.

Be gracious and polite when people do offer you advice, but don't fall into the trap of thinking that you *have* to listen to them. And it doesn't matter if they are insistent with their views – if their advice doesn't feel right, then trust your instincts. So, as much as they are insistent with their advice, feel free to be equally as insistent in saying 'Thanks, but no thanks'.

Make sure you speak to a careers advisor, who is professionally trained and should be impartial.

Remember the decision should always be yours. After all, you will live with the decision you make – whoever is advising you won't!

# Section 1 summary: Introduction

Apprenticeships are an exciting and important option – you have done well to consider them.

- Great employers are embracing apprenticeships.
- You can now access almost any career via an apprenticeship.
- Governments around the world are committed to supporting apprenticeships.
- Doing an apprenticeship is highly likely to boost your earning power.
- Apprenticeships fit the needs of the fast changing economy of the 21st century.

This guidebook is here to help you understand apprenticeships, whether they might be right for you and how you go about getting them. Crucially, it will equip you for the discussions you are likely to have with family, friends and teachers who are advising you (remember: there may be people who want to be helpful but, because they do not have the latest information, may be less helpful than they hope).

Use this book in whatever way you want, and keep coming back to dip into the parts that feel most relevant and useful to you.

## APPRENTICE CASE STUDY: JANELLE RAPHANAHANE

Janelle really didn't know what she wanted to do as she came to the end of school. She was pretty sure she didn't want to go to university, which would involve moving out of home, incurring debt and relying on her mum's financial support – particularly as she doesn't even like studying!

Being nagged by her mum, she researched options and signed up to webinars. Having figured out that she wanted an office career, she began to home in on finance apprenticeships – after all, she liked numbers and maths. Janelle then specifically researched finance apprenticeships and identified just one that sounded what she was looking for, with Grant Thornton.

'I really went for it, doing as much research as I could on the company and the programme. The assessment process was tough, with interviews (some of which were awkward self-filmed answers) and assignments, but I felt prepared. I also made contact via LinkedIn with one of the firm's partners, which really boosted my confidence and my sense that I could belong there.'

And it worked out: Janelle received an unconditional offer for the apprenticeship before her friends had even completed their UCAS forms. She was able to relax and fully enjoy her last year at school – and to her pleasant surprise, she got 3 Bs at A level.

She is now six months into her Accountancy Apprenticeship, specialising in Audit. It is a five-year Level 7 scheme, and she will be a fully qualified Accountant at the end of it. She will not have paid any fees and will have earned (very well) for all of those five years. Whatever she wants to do next – carry on, take a year out to travel, or even move career – she will be extremely well placed.

'No one had told me about apprenticeships before. The way you learn in an apprenticeship suits me: I have learned bit by bit through experience, and can now really feel that I am getting on top of the work and am able to contribute at meetings – it's really exciting. I love going to visit clients as we work with some really cool companies, including a gaming company and one who provides technical services to one of the world's biggest entertainment organisations.'

Janelle says how exciting – and a bit scary – it was to join the world of work straight from school. 'I thought the working day finished at 4.30pm – they were very nice in the way they told me it was, in fact, 5.30pm!' She also says how helpful and fun it is to be on a programme with other people who are a similar age and just starting out, with lots of social events and perks.

One piece of advice she is keen to pass on: 'There is a lot to do in an apprenticeship: your work AND your studies. You have to get good at time management!'

She says that A levels and getting to uni really are not the only option. 'Don't feel you need to do what your teachers tell you – do your own homework. I've got friends at good universities also studying accountancy. One has dropped out already and is looking for an apprenticeship, and another comes to me for advice on the technical content of accountancy, even though they're the ones doing the degree. I also get to go and visit them and enjoy the social life. I'm really not missing out. I'm so glad I made the choice I did and went for it.'

## EMPLOYER CASE STUDY: ARC GROUP LONDON

Arc Group London is a SME (small- and medium-sized enterprise) within the construction industry made up of various divisions such as: waterproofing, M&E (mechanical and electrical), fire compliance, property services (e.g. fitting kitchens and bathrooms) and more large-scale capital projects such as extensions and refurbishment works to schools and public buildings.

They offer apprenticeships at all levels, from Levels 2 and 3 in trade occupations such as electrics, plumbing, roofing and carpentry all the way up to degree apprenticeships in Quantity Surveying, Business Management and Design & Build. Some 18% of their team are apprentices – a significant proportion that demonstrates just how valuable apprenticeships are for them.

'There is a massive shortage of skills in our industry. As a business we understand how vital apprenticeships are to address this. Without our apprentices we wouldn't be able to grow as a business.'

So says Amy Packer, the company's Social Value Manager, responsible for helping Arc fulfil its requirements to add value to the local communities in which it works, which includes managing their apprenticeship programme. It's no surprise that Amy is an enthusiast – she began her career as an apprentice herself (doing business administration) within the construction industry. She worked her way up through different divisions within construction and eventually found her current role: she is living proof of how apprenticeships can take you from being a school leaver to an influential member of management within nine years.

She notes that apprenticeships are a great way for people to develop their skills, because the learning and qualification part of an apprenticeship validates and reinforces how the person is growing professionally – something that might otherwise get lost. 'Often people don't realise that what they are doing in the workplace is as important as it is; the apprenticeship allows them to fully understand their role, while also preparing them for the role they are going to move into next. The fact that they can ask questions, there and then, from their colleagues and peers, means that their learning is in real time and completely relevant.'

On top of that, she points out, you don't have university fees to cover and are gaining experience in the world of work.

Her advice to those thinking about whether they are right for an apprenticeship is clear: 'You need to have commitment and personal drive. You need to be able to motivate yourself for the studying side of the apprenticeship as well as the work side, which means you need to enjoy what you are doing.'

She also has useful advice on how to maximise your chances of success in an apprenticeship: 'Don't be shy about asking questions! Don't fall into the trap of thinking that you shouldn't "bother" senior people who you think might be "too busy" – the job of a manager IS to help develop people starting out, and they love to be asked questions and to help, not least because it allows them to validate their own experience and to share their knowledge and experience.'

# Section 2
# The power of
# apprenticeships

# Introduction to Section 2: The power of apprenticeships

This section explains what makes an apprenticeship such a powerful way to start your career, and how this is being increasingly recognised by more and more people.

In this section we explore:

- why apprenticeships work
- the sheer breadth of careers you can get into via an apprenticeship
- why employers increasingly value apprenticeships
- why young people are choosing apprenticeships
- why the Government supports apprenticeships
- why schools and colleges are increasingly supportive of apprenticeships.

# 2.1 Why apprenticeships work

The way an apprenticeship works means you learn – really learn – how to do a job.

Imagine you want to learn how to do something new, let's say, how to bake a cake.

Picture the scene: you are set up in a kitchen ready to go, with your baking teacher standing next to you. Apron on, mixing bowls and cake tins on the worktop, ingredients laid out. You are ready, so is your teacher.

What happens next?

Maybe your teacher says: 'Don't worry about all this stuff in front of us. Instead, take your apron off, go to your desk and read a book on cake baking for a few hours.' The book could be useful, explaining why the ingredients work together and what chemical processes are happening when the mixture cooks, and so on. Maybe your teacher will recommend that you watch some videos of cake baking or read the blogs of famous cake bakers. All of this could be interesting and cover lots of stuff you didn't know before.

But it would be a strange way to learn how to bake a cake.

Strange, but in fact this is the traditional model for 'education': you learn *about* a subject *from* another person, the teacher, supplemented by other material you passively receive, such as books, articles and videos. You (supposedly) absorb lots of knowledge, with only a few practical skills included. You then take a written exam that tests your memory more than anything else. And then much of what you have learned 'evaporates' soon after (you may recognise this from your academic studies at school).

Or would you prefer it if... you got started, there and then, to actually bake a cake, guided and helped by a 'teacher'. They would show you which ingredients to use and how much, showing you how to weigh the flour and how to mix the ingredients. Then they would hand over to you so you can give it a go yourself. If you don't quite get it right first time, it's okay, because they are on hand to show you how to do it the right way.

As you get more comfortable and confident, your teacher starts to tell you more about different techniques and approaches. They might start sharing stories from their cake-baking career to bring it to life and to open your thinking. In turn, you may start to ask questions, prompted by what you are doing and learning in the moment.

This option blends different ways of learning: the practical skills, some of the background knowledge and some of the things you need to get right in your approach. It is this blend that makes it so powerful: the practical learning enhances your knowledge, and your knowledge enhances your practical skills.

This example is learning how to bake a cake, but could have been any skill or 'know-how' you have recently learned or that you have taught to someone else. The same principle applies: *People naturally want to learn by doing, because this is how the human brain is wired to learn.*

There is a brilliant book called *The Secret of our Success* by Joseph Henrich which explains exactly how humans learn from each other (and have done so for tens of thousands of years). Henrich shows that this ability to learn from each other, in a practical and immediate way, is the reason why human beings have been so much more successful than other animals in controlling our environment. He shows that our ability to learn is, in fact, more important than the size of our brains or our opposable thumbs.

People learn best with the support and guidance of someone who they trust to help them: someone who has done it before; someone who is prepared to take the time to show them; someone who has their best interests at heart; someone who will watch over them as they take their tentative first steps, correcting them 'little and often' as they become increasingly confident and independent; someone who will encourage them through the fun bits and the tricky bits alike. This kind of learning tends to stick because it lodges in both the 'thinking' and the 'doing' parts of our brains.

This is exactly what an apprenticeship is, and this is why it is so powerful: instead of learning *about* the job you are going to do, you learn *how to do it*, using all the parts of your brain that enable you to learn – really learn – how to do something.

In an apprenticeship

- whenever you learn something, you can put it into practice straightaway, making you better at your job immediately ('theory with a purpose')
- you get a coach who sees how you are getting on objectively, advises you and guides you through issues and problems
- you have a line manager who gives you clear instructions before you undertake a task and then gives you clear and insightful feedback afterwards
- you have permission to ask any question you want, knowing that people expect you to ask these questions *because* you are an apprentice
- you will learn the habits of reflection and active learning, disciplines that will accelerate and enhance your prospects for the rest of your life.

It is not that an apprenticeship is just one more way to learn how to do a job – it is the very best way to learn how to do a job. That's why it has been the tried and tested way for occupations to bring new people into their world, since the days of the Ancient Greeks (and probably before!).

# 2.2 Almost all careers are now accessible through an apprenticeship

It used to be that apprenticeships were only available for manual occupations, such as construction and manufacturing. Often they were seen as being for young people who 'couldn't' do other things, as though other options were 'better' (by the way: jobs in construction and manufacturing are now highly prized occupations that command good salaries).

However, the status and role of apprenticeships has changed beyond all recognition since those days. There is now almost no occupation for which there is not an apprenticeship route. And when you consider that an apprenticeship cannot exist here in the UK without the buy-in of at least ten significant employers, you know for sure that apprenticeships are a serious option for all sectors and all occupations.

You can now become a fully qualified doctor, solicitor, management consultant, quantity surveyor or engineer via an apprenticeship.

If anyone says that apprenticeships are 'second rate' or 'beneath you', politely point them to the Institute for Apprenticeships & Technical Education website to show them just how wrong they are (instituteforapprenticeships.org). And share with them what you find in this book and in your other research. People giving you this advice will almost certainly be out-of-date – it's not their fault (usually!), but you can and should definitely put them right.

So, let's have a quick skim across the world of apprenticeships.

If you like working with your hands, there are dozens of apprenticeships you might be interested in. Some have been around for a long time, like electrician, plumber or carpenter, while others are newer, such as lifting technician, smart meter installer and acoustics technician. While demand for roles can ebb and flow, there is a chronic shortage of qualified people in these domains, and you normally need to have formal qualifications to enter them, so an apprenticeship is perfect.

For those who like to be outdoors, working with nature and/or animals there are lots of apprenticeships too. You can become a veterinary technician, a tree surgeon (arborist is the official term), a golf course greenkeeper, a horse or dog groomer or a countryside ranger.

If you want to get into the 'professions', such as becoming a lawyer or accountant, you no longer have to go to university and get a degree; there is now a ladder of apprenticeships that take you all the way to being fully qualified within a few years, getting paid all the while you are qualifying.

You can also become a doctor and nurse via apprenticeships now, with the first doctor apprentices starting in early 2024 (by the way: you will be just as qualified as the doctor or nurse who followed a degree course!). Apprenticeships are a great way into dentistry or pharmacology, as well as into other medical occupations such as radiography and occupational therapy.

If you want to work in the health and care sector but don't want to be medical, there are lots of care apprenticeships available, whether that's looking after and guiding children or providing support for adults who are vulnerable.

You might love working with computers and see that this is where a long-term career in the 21st century lies. Well, there are tons of apprenticeships in this particular field, from being an IT technician helping organisations out with their day-to-day IT requirements, being a software programmer or tester, or using IT to work with and get the most out of data (brilliant if you love logic and maths).

If you are creative but worry that getting into a viable career will take contacts and luck – well, there are now many apprenticeships available because creative organisations realise that great employees come from all sorts of backgrounds. Whether you want to work in theatre or television, or become a journalist, or work on special effects, or create computer games or get into arts and crafts – there's an apprenticeship for you.

If you like to be part of a team making and building things, whether that's in a factory or out 'on site,' or maintaining and looking after things once they have been built, then there are dozens (literally!) of engineering apprenticeships. There are apprenticeships in advanced manufacturing, in construction, in transport (from railways to aviation) and in the water and energy industries – including working in nuclear power! And new apprenticeships are on the way in green energy.

Sales and marketing are a great place to start and build a career: they are professions that will *always* be needed, come what may, with lots of variety and opportunities to progress fast while being creative and always at the sharp end of business. Unsurprisingly, there are lots of apprenticeships here too, from digital marketing (using social media and websites to drive brand awareness and sales) to advertising to full-on sales and PR (public relations).

If you like to create amazing experiences and enjoyment for people, there are apprenticeships for you as well. Apprenticeships in hair and beauty are well established and have been a vital part of their industries for decades. So too are apprenticeships in hospitality, whether that's working in a fancy restaurant or learning how to keep the punters happy in a pub. If you like being active and want to help others to do the same, then apprenticeships in sports coaching and personal training could be right for you.

Perhaps you are driven by keeping people safe and secure? Guess what… there are 18 apprenticeships, ranging from becoming a police officer to being a fire safety inspector.

You've probably got the picture by now: apprenticeships are available in every walk of life.

Go to https://occupational-maps.instituteforapprenticeships.org, where you will be able to explore the full range of apprenticeships available and discover how you can build a career through them.

# 2.3 Employers see the value of apprenticeships

There is no better proof of the rapidly growing recognition of apprenticeships than the number of 'blue chip' (large, well-established, financially sound) employers who have swung their recruitment programmes towards apprenticeships.

Just ten years ago, the likes of Google, KPMG, Goldman Sachs, Shell, WPP and Barclays offered almost no apprenticeships. Today, these companies are recruiting huge numbers of new employees through apprenticeship schemes, as are Government departments, local authorities, charities, start-ups, mid-sized firms and other employers of all shapes and sizes.

To give you a sense of just how many different employers employ apprentices, here are some of the employers who got shortlisted at the National Apprenticeships Award in 2022:

Mega employers (those employing more than 5,000 people):

- Atkins (atkinsglobal.com) – engineering and design firm
- BBC (bbc.co.uk) – national broadcaster
- Go-Ahead Group (go-ahead.com) – public transport company, running buses and trains throughout the UK
- Greene King (greeneking.co.uk) – pub retailer and brewer, running over 2,700 pubs, restaurants and hotels in the UK
- Howdens Joinery Group (howdens.com) – one of the biggest companies making and installing kitchens and other joinery in the UK
- IBM UK (ibm.com) – international IT and data company
- Royal Air Force (raf.mod.uk) – no explanation required!
- Royal Mail Group (royalmail.com) – delivers letters and parcels around the UK and internationally
- Travis Perkins (travisperkins.co.uk) – provides building goods and services to construction companies across the country.

Large employers (organisations employing between 250 and 5,000 people):

- Chesterfield Royal Hospital NHS Foundation Trust – a major NHS hospital in Derbyshire
- Flagship Group – social housing organisation that builds, maintains and lets homes in East Anglia
- KMF Group –Staffordshire-based sheet metal engineering and metal fabrication company
- Labcorp – Yorkshire company that helps to develop new medicines through clinical trials
- MTR Elizabeth line – the company that built and operates the new crossrail in London
- Pennon Group – environmental utility infrastructure company that owns South West Water and other utility companies
- RSM UK – leading audit, tax and consultancy firm based in the South East of England but operating globally
- SiemensGamesa Renewable Energy – Hull-based manufacturer of the largest wind turbines in the UK
- WEC Group – manufacturing and engineering company based in Darwen, Lancashire.

Small- and medium-sized employers (up to 250 employees):

- Adopstar – data-driven digital advertising agency on the Devon/Dorset border
- Dental22 – award-winning dental practice in Nottinghamshire
- Intelect – engineering company based in the north-east but operating across the UK
- JLES Group – civil engineering company specialising in new roads and sewage pipes, based in Manchester but operating across the UK
- Metalcraft – precision engineering and manufacturing firm based in Nottinghamshire
- R&W Civil Engineering – Southampton-based engineering firm specialising in highways

- Staffordshire & Stoke-on-Trent Integrated Care System – bringing together NHS and social care for this part of the West Midlands
- Tribosonics – cutting-edge Sheffield firm specialising in high end sensors for the energy industry
- Troup Bywaters + Anders – engineering consultancy firm based in London.

The variety and range of these employers – who are just the tip of the iceberg – are huge: all sectors, all parts of the country, all sizes. In total, nearly 70,000 employers in the UK in 2020/21 employed an apprentice.

There are six reasons why employers in the UK have got 'the apprenticeship bug'.

i.   Great way to find talent and skills.
ii.  Diversify the workforce.
iii. Extra support.
iv.  FOMO!
v.   By employers, for employers.
vi.  Financial incentives.

## 1. A great way to find talent & skills

Apprenticeships work for employers as a way of finding talented people and for building skills. Around the world, employers are finding it hard to get the people who can do the jobs they need them to do, so they are desperately trying to find better ways to staff their companies than through traditional recruitment or graduate programmes. In the UK, employers have faced additional problems since Brexit (UK's decision to leave the European Union came into effect in January 2020), as established pools of people from within the EU were suddenly cut off. This means that employers are now looking for 'homegrown' talent, and are prepared to invest in them in order to build the skills they need. Many employers, once they have started an apprenticeship programme, never look back, and put apprenticeships at the heart of the recruitment strategy.

**❝❞ The big question we had when we began our apprenticeship programme ten years ago was: could they help us generate revenue? The short answer is a resounding "yes".**

*Jenny Taylor MBE, Leader of IBM UK's Early Professional Programmes (Foundation)*

## 2. Diversify their workforce

Employers like apprenticeships because, importantly, they help diversify their workforce. Diversity is a huge issue for companies large and small: they recognise that if they want to come up with successful products and services, and to understand their customers and users better, they need to ensure their employees come from a wide range of backgrounds.

**❝❞ Apprenticeships are also a really effective way for us to hire people from diverse backgrounds – we value the benefits that difference can bring.**

*Jamie Pemberton-Legg, Head of Apprenticeships, BT Group*

Because of the structure of apprenticeship programmes (see 'Extra support' below), they give confidence to employers to take on people from diverse backgrounds, and similarly they give confidence to people from diverse backgrounds to apply to organisations that they might not otherwise have done.

**❝❞ Our founder was passionate about the opportunity agenda, giving people who wouldn't otherwise have the opportunity a chance. Apprenticeships are a really tangible way in which Starbucks here in the UK is making that a reality. People who start as a barista know they can rapidly develop through apprenticeships to being a store manager.**

*Anita Desai, Opportunity, Inclusion and Wellbeing Advisor, Starbucks UK*

## 3. Extra support

With apprenticeships, employers are supported when they want to take on someone new – they know they have the training provider to support them and Government backing. This gives them the reassurance and support to proceed.

**❝❞ As an employer, you have the confidence that someone else is helping you with the training load. You have the confidence to employ a young person as an apprentice because you know that there is that extra support from the training provider.'**

*Louis Warner, Chief Operating Officer, Founders Factory*

## 4. FOMO!

Employers don't want to lose out to competitors: they see their competitors using apprenticeships to recruit brilliant young talent and upskill their staff, they see other organisations winning awards and they see the growing number of case studies showing off just how good apprenticeships are. They get FOMO – they hate the thought that their competitors are succeeding by doing something they are not. Which is good news for anyone interested in doing an apprenticeship.

> **In a sector where there is a simple shortage of people who can do what we need, we are competing hard for talent. Apprenticeships are strategically essential, and we want to benefit to the maximum.**
>
> *Craig Brown, Apprenticeship & Learning Advisor, Henry Boot*

## 5. By employers, for employers

Apprenticeships are 'by employers, for employers': increasingly employers are seeing that because every apprenticeship programme (called a Standard) has had to be designed by at least ten employers like them, this is as close as they can get to a ready-made programme that's right for them. Consequently, they believe in the content of the programmes and believe in the process. It helps that often some of the employers who have helped shape the programmes are some of the biggest, most renowned employers in their sector – so other employers naturally look up to what they have done and want to get involved.

> **Apprenticeship Standards are now really good. The mix between the theory and practice, learning from real people in the world of work, is a powerful combination.'**
>
> *Nell Weller, Consultant and former Managing Partner, TB+A*

## 6. Financial incentives

The Government has made it financially attractive for employers to use apprenticeships through the 'Apprenticeship Levy'. The levy requires firms that employ more than 100 people to spend money on apprenticeship training (if they choose not to, they have to pay an additional tax). The Government also helps those firms that do not have enough employees to have to pay the Apprenticeship Levy by giving them a 95% subsidy for apprenticeship training fees. Indeed, for the smallest companies (with fewer than 50 employees) they fund the entire cost of the apprenticeship training. They also offer £1,000 to employers when they take on an apprentice who is 16–18 years old (or 19–24 years old if they have had an Education, Health and Care plan and/or have been in care).

# 2.4 Young people see the value of apprenticeships

Perhaps most importantly from your point of view, more and more young people like you are seeing the value of doing an apprenticeship. Almost half of the people registering on UCAS are now considering an apprenticeship. In 2021/22 nearly 184,000 young people between the ages of 16 and 24 started an apprenticeship.

There are five main reasons for doing an apprenticeship that young people focus on:

1. accelerated career start
2. money
3. learning that feels real and relevant
4. personal growth
5. the qualification.

## 1. Accelerated career start

**It made a huge difference that I started my career so early, aged 17... I had a four-year head start on my friends who went to university; four years in which I not only learned a lot and got my qualification, but I also earned and got promotions. I was way ahead of my mates when they finished uni.**

*George Eiloart, qualified apprentice*

An apprenticeship straight after school means you can get your career up and running as soon as possible. An apprentice has 'permission' and the opportunity to learn from lots of different people and situations in a short space of time. They have many opportunities to make a positive impression on lots of colleagues, which in turn can lead to promotions and even more opportunities.

**It really gets you those early years of experience which provide such a massive head start. I'm 26, but I have double the years' work experience compared to my friends who went to uni.**

*Olly Newman, qualified apprentice*

People who do an apprenticeship and get a head start over people who went to uni can, as Olly has done, maintain that gap – because once you have a year or two's work experience, most employers do not care at all if you have a degree – and those who are starting their career with a degree find that they still have to get the same amount of work experience to compete: the degree on its own just does not count for that much.

**❝❞ I haven't yet completed my apprenticeship and already my company are talking about me taking on higher roles.**

*Jack Bonfield, apprentice*

## 2. Money

People who have done apprenticeships point out two ways in which they are financially better off.

i.   They haven't incurred the costs and debt that comes with going to university (unless you are lucky enough to have parents who can support you the whole way).

ii.  They have been earning money from the get-go.

'I wanted to get out, earn some money, and get going,' says Olly Newman about his decision to opt for an apprenticeship while all his friends were staying on to do A levels.

Even if you are on the lowest possible apprenticeship wage (assuming it's a full-time role) you will get £858 into your bank account every month. If you are earning the average apprenticeship starting salary of £21,000 a year, that monthly income goes up to £1,525 a month (a little less than £21,000 divided by 12 months, because once you are earning £12,570 a year or more you start to pay tax).

Given that on average a student leaves university with debt of £43,000 and that the average earnings of an apprentice over three years are £63,000, the decision to go to university can add up (on average) to a total 'cost' of £106,000.

While money may not buy happiness, it is a tangible token that you are contributing and making your own way in the world – which can be very satisfying. As the comedian Chris Rock said, 'Wealth is not about having a lot of money; it's about having a lot of options.'

For example, earning money while you are still young means you can start to save earlier – several of the people who are case studies in this book are buying houses while still in their twenties because of what they have been able to save from the first few years of their careers.

**❝❞ And having money can be fun: 'When you do go to see your mates at uni, it's quite nice to be the one buying the drinks!'**

*George Eiloart, qualified apprentice*

Of course, you may be concerned that by doing an apprenticeship you won't be able to get jobs that are as well paid as if you were a graduate. It's really important to know that this is no longer always true: a degree does not guarantee a good salary.

If you apply yourself conscientiously to your job and your apprenticeship studies, it is likely that whatever wage you start on will go up, sometimes while you are still an apprentice. Often there is a pay rise on completion of your apprenticeship, and many people who qualify as an apprentice see their wages rise strongly, so that by their mid-twenties they may be earning as much as those in the same career with a degree.

## 3. Learning that feels real & relevant

A number of people who have done apprenticeships talk about what a source of joy and relief it was to them to be able to move away from academic studies. For many, the way in which they are required to learn at school and university just does not work for them.

Sometimes this is because it does not feel relevant or meaningful, or they don't like how teachers approach them, or it may be because they are neurodivergent in a way that makes academic learning difficult, for example if they have dyslexia or experience attention deficit disorder, or it may be because of a combination of these things.

For people in this situation, to be told that your 'best' or 'only' route forward is yet more academic study in the same style, whether at A levels or on into university, can be a bit depressing.

Therefore, to discover that there is a route that can lead to a great career, that is respectable and that does NOT require just academic study is something of a revelation. Of course, apprenticeships do require some element of theory, especially degree apprenticeships –

but that theory is directly relevant to the job that the apprentice is doing and so does not feel as purely academic in the same way as school or uni work.

**❝❞ I am dyslexic, which meant I always found academic work tricky. I knew university would not have worked with how I learn. Even as my school pushed everyone down the UCAS route, my parents were really supportive as I looked for apprenticeships, as I knew they would work better for me.**

*Aidan Lancaster, qualifed apprentice now doing higher apprenticeship*

## 4. Personal growth

Apprentices often say how they have developed and grown as human beings, and believe that they wouldn't have experienced that as much if they had stayed inside the education system. The difference is that at school or university things are done for you (you are the 'customer', as it were), whereas in the world of work you have to forge your own way and make your own decisions as you grow into becoming an employee, not a student.

This can be daunting, but also exciting and incredibly rewarding.

**❝❞ I was very young to be entering a professional environment; I had to grow up so quickly, surrounded by my colleagues and clients. I was constantly out of my comfort zone – but in return, my confidence grew really quickly.**

*Shayla Crane, qualified apprentice*

**❝❞ My character has really been built through this apprenticeship.**

*Jack Bonfield, apprentice*

## 5. The qualification

**❝❞ Apprenticeships combine practical, on-the-job training with study: you have the opportunity to learn while bringing in a wage, working alongside experienced staff and gaining skills unique to the workplace, as well as getting an increasingly well-respected qualification.**

*Muhammed Lateef, qualified apprentice*

Qualifications do two key things: 1) they show someone who has never met you before that you are at a **required level** (or above) in relation to work-related attributes and 2) that you **care** enough about those attributes to have gone to the trouble of getting a qualification that shows that.

It is important, therefore, that you can get a rigorous qualification, even if you have opted not to go the 'traditional' or expected route of university. The apprenticeship qualification is exactly this, a rigorous qualification: it is 'protected' in law, which means no one can call a training programme an 'apprenticeship' unless they are following the formal Government programme (they can be actually prosecuted if they do). This in turn means that the qualification and brand is protected – and is becoming increasingly recognised and respected.

It is also increasingly common that apprenticeships now come with their own graduation ceremonies, providing the opportunity for that all important picture of you 'graduating' for your loved ones to proudly display at home on the mantelpiece.

Of course, those doing degree apprenticeships get a degree as well. A growing number of people see this as the 'ultimate' tertiary qualification: the status and rigour of a degree, plus the applied learning and work experience of an apprenticeship. For many young people, how everything comes together in one package is unique and powerful.

**❝❞ I got a free degree, no student debt, and really valuable work experience.**

*Emma Nolan, qualified degree apprentice*

# 2.5  Governments see the value of apprenticeships

So: apprenticeships are a uniquely powerful way to learn how to do a job and get started in all kinds of careers, which is why a growing number of employers are using them.

The Government also plays a crucial role: they run the system as a whole, making sure that larger employers fund the training for apprenticeships and subsidising smaller employers so they can participate; they make sure that the qualifications are robust and relevant; and they make sure that training providers are run properly and (through OFSTED) are delivering quality programmes.

So while the Government is currently supportive of apprenticeships, you may be wondering how likely it is that this could change?

Well, nothing in politics is certain. But politicians know that the UK is behind other countries in terms of productivity (i.e. how good we are as a country at getting stuff done): the Office for National Statistics reported in January 2023 that the UK's average output per worker was 16% less than the G7 group of countries excluding Japan (i.e. the USA, France, Germany, Canada, Italy).

The Government believes that this is, in large part, because of poor skills. They are, therefore, very keen indeed on initiatives that help employers acquire more and better skills. Apprenticeships fit the bill perfectly, as they focus on the latest skills required to get the job done, across all sectors and for all organisations across the entire economy. In other words, apprenticeships are an obvious and important solution for a really difficult problem that all politicians want to solve.

Efforts by UK governments since the start of the 21st century to boost apprenticeships are working: according to the House of Commons Library (pretty much the most official source of these sorts of statistics) in the year 2000 there were 165,000 people who started apprenticeships in the UK. By 2010 that number had gone up to 280,000. It then reached around 500,000 people starting an apprenticeship every year pretty consistently from 2011 to 2017.

In 2017, reforms to improve the long-term quality of apprenticeships caused the number of new apprenticeships to dip as employers got used to the changes involved.

Then, just as numbers were starting to go back up, the global pandemic, Covid-19, hit, which meant that employers battened down the hatches and recruited fewer people all round, including apprentices. Nevertheless, by 2021 the number of new apprenticeship starts was still strong, at just over 300,000 (and still comfortably higher than it had been ten years before), but obviously down from the high of 500,000.

The estimates for 2022 are that 350,000 people began apprenticeships, suggesting that numbers are going back up as the economy normalises.

Here's what some politicians say about apprenticeships.

The Secretary of State for Education at the time I am writing this book is Gillian Keegan. She makes the decisions for the Government about how it funds and structures all education: schools, universities and skills programmes, like apprenticeships. In an interview on LBC radio in December 2022, she said: 'I left school at 16 and did an apprenticeship in a car factory. It was a brilliant way to get into the workplace. We need to make sure there is more of that on offer for more people.' She also said, 'It's a fifty grand decision – one of the three biggest decisions you make in your life.' Why does she think apprenticeships are so good? 'You get paid, you don't have to pay back your tuition fees, you start earning earlier.'

But what if there's a change of government? Could this support disappear? It is possible – but unlikely. Here's what the shadow education minister, Bridget Phillipson, of the Labour Party (the most likely alternative government at the next election) said recently: 'Labour has set out an ambitious plan to create 100,000 new apprenticeship opportunities for young people harnessing their skills and capabilities to fuel our economic recovery post-pandemic.' What is interesting about this is how she has made the link explicit between apprenticeships and the overall economic health of the country.

It's the same story for many other politicians too. Here's what the Skills Minister for Scotland said in 2022: 'When it comes to supporting sustainable skills through workforce development or providing opportunities for young people, we know that apprenticeships work.'

In short, apprenticeships are popular with politicians because they believe that they are good for the economy, good for the young people who do them and good for employers.

Indeed, the opposition parties often like to bash the party in power for not doing enough to promote apprenticeships.

If you search the news for apprenticeships, you will find lots of debate and controversy – but it is all about how to make apprenticeships work better and how to encourage more apprenticeships (both from employers and among young people). There is no one saying, 'We need to have fewer apprenticeships'.

## 💡 Interesting idea: Apprenticeships are a global phenomenon

Apprenticeships are increasingly common around the world. This means anyone undertaking an apprenticeship is part of a growing global movement.

**Germany**, **Austria** and **Switzerland** have long-established apprenticeship systems, in which a majority of young people do some form of apprenticeship:

- 60% of Germans at the age of 16 will go into apprenticeships via the 'dual system'
- 70% of young Swiss people opt for apprenticeships over the academic path on completion of compulsory schooling
- 40% of Austrian teenagers opt for apprenticeships.

Ever wondered why their economies are so successful...?

In the **United States** the Federal budget to support apprenticeships went up tenfold from 2015 to 2022, and the number of people starting an apprenticeship is now more than 600,000 a year, in diverse occupations such as advanced manufacturing and IT, as well as traditional apprenticeships in construction and trades.

Around the world there is growing recognition that a degree is not the be all and end all. An article in the prestigious *Harvard Business Review* from Spring 2023 said: 'Some hiring managers think that a degree serves as a good proxy for capabilities such as collaborating well, taking initiative and thinking critically. There's virtually no evidence to support that notion.'

Major US firms moving away from hiring based on a college degree to hiring on the basis of skills include Microsoft, Google, Apple, General Motors, Accenture, Aon and IBM. Where these huge global firms lead, others are following.

Many European countries are now introducing or increasing their apprenticeship programmes. For example, in **France**, reforms in 2018 meant the number of entry level apprenticeships per year went from just under 180,000 to 280,000, and the number of degree apprenticeships nearly quadrupled from 118,000 a year to 443,000 a year. The impact has been significant, with a reduction in youth unemployment of nearly 20%.

A growing number of **African** countries are formalising and providing government support for apprenticeships, with **South Africa** explicitly copying the German model. **China** is beginning to pilot formal apprenticeships too, albeit starting from a low base of 500,000 in 2020 (as many as the UK, but in a population 50 times bigger).

The World Economic Forum in 2017 put the case for apprenticeships around the world well: 'A well-tested path to tackle skills shortages is apprenticeships. Countries that have long-established apprenticeship models have low youth unemployment rates, demonstrating their success. They keep pace with changes in technology, work practices and market dynamics. And they combine the classroom with workplace training so young people acquire relevant skills via apprenticeships.'

# 2.6 Schools and colleges see the value of apprenticeships

If you have got this book through your school or college, then you know that they are taking apprenticeships seriously – at least seriously enough to invest in this book!

For years, many schools have promoted university as the 'best' route for 'most' students.

There are lots of reasons for this: most teachers went to university, and it is human nature that they may believe that what worked for them will work for you; schools (and therefore teachers) are judged on how many of their students go on to university – they are not judged (yet) on other possible choices students might take (albeit degree apprenticeships now count towards their targets). It is also arguably easier for them to support students to apply for university: there are only 160 to apply to in the UK and just one form (UCAS) to complete.

Apprenticeships on the other hand… well, they feel like hard work to advise on if you are a teacher: there are, after all, 1,000,000 different employers across the country, doing a bewildering variety of things, all hiring at different times throughout the year, with each local area having different employers, with over 600 different apprenticeship programmes at different levels, where each employer and each apprenticeship could vary hugely.

On top of this, very few teachers have done apprenticeships themselves, so it is even harder for them to be confident and knowledgeable when it comes to advising you.

But times are changing and schools and colleges are now beginning to take apprenticeships much more seriously, for four reasons.

i. For all the reasons outlined elsewhere in this book, apprenticeships really work as a post-school option.

ii. Schools and colleges now have to tell you about apprenticeships, legally. In 2017, the Government introduced something called 'The Baker Clause' (named after the retired Education Minister, Ken Baker, who has always been a big supporter of vocational skills); this legally requires schools and colleges to introduce their students to apprenticeships. And in 2022 the Government strengthened this clause by specifying exactly what schools and colleges have to do. The upshot is that schools and colleges are now actively searching for ways to introduce you to the whole world of apprenticeships.

iii. From Autumn 2023, it is possible to apply for apprenticeships through UCAS (The Universities and Colleges Admissions Service). And from Autumn 2024 it will be possible to apply for apprenticeships while also applying for university places. While the process of applying for an apprenticeship via UCAS is more complicated than applying for a place at university, at least it has made it into the system, and is visible to teachers.

iv. Degree apprenticeships count towards school league tables – which means that schools and teachers are now incentivised to push this route as much as traditional university degrees.

All of the above is great news – it means that teachers now have an extra reason to do the right thing and ensure students can find out about apprenticeships. But this is all pretty new for most teachers, so they are still finding their way.

Listen carefully to what they say but ask them lots of questions, and in doing so you will help them to help you. And if they have not read this book yet, tell them to!

# Section 2 summary:
# The power of apprenticeships

Apprenticeships are a great way to learn how to get good at a job. This is because how you learn in an apprenticeship goes 'with the grain' of how our brains are designed to learn – by *doing*, with an expert by our side (like baking a cake).

Almost all careers are now available through an apprenticeship, both traditional 'trades' and those that were previously only available to those with a degree. Whatever you are interested in, there is almost certainly a selection of apprenticeships for you.

Employers see the value of apprenticeships. Whether large or small, whatever the sector, more and more employers are using apprenticeships because they work – they help them diversify their workforce and they are designed by employers, for employers. It also helps that the Government provides financial support for apprenticeships.

Perhaps most importantly, young people themselves attest to the power and value of doing an apprenticeship. It helps them get a rapid start to their career, it is financially attractive, for some it means a way to leave academic study while keeping hold of aspiration, it can have a deep and beneficial personal impact – and it still leads to a respected qualification.

Not surprisingly, the Government sees their value too – they are their 'best bet' to solve the skills crisis that the country faces. In turn, schools and colleges (in part because they now legally have to) are spending more time and effort on explaining apprenticeships.

### APPRENTICE CASE STUDY: OLLY NEWMAN

'I thought that the decision I was taking back when I was 16 was a decision for life,' says Olly Newman, as he looks back ten years to when he started his first apprenticeship in Building Services at leading engineering firm TB+A.

'It was really daunting at that age, with all my mates staying on to do A levels, to be getting on a train to go work in the City. Of course, it wasn't a decision for life – although I'm still at the same company I did my apprenticeship with – you just have to examine the pros and cons of your options and pick the one which is best for you, as far as you can tell at the time.'

For Olly, that meant leaving school as quickly as he could: 'I wanted to get out, earn some money, and get going.' He applied for an apprenticeship with TB+A, with whom he had done some work experience the previous summer, which itself came about through a family friend. He took the opportunities that he found in front of him – there was no grand plan, but so far, it is working out: he has just been promoted to Project Associate.

His advice to people still at school considering whether to do an apprenticeship, go to uni or do something else is to realise that a job is both daunting and exciting. 'Of course I had to learn the technical skills required for the job and for the qualification, just like in any career, but I also had to get really good at time management – it's a lot to do when you're starting off in your first job: starting a new job and getting a robust qualification.'

He also points out that you should not expect doing an apprenticeship to be anything like school: it doesn't always run smoothly – it's the real world after all! – and you have to speak out and ask for help if something isn't happening that should be. 'Sometimes information didn't flow well between my training provider, me and my line manager – so you have to be sharp to make sure things happen, be organised, and not wait for it to be done for you.'

But he is clear that if you've got an idea of what you want to do – even if it's not fully formed – then there is no better option than an apprenticeship. 'It really gets you those early years of experience which provide such a massive head start. I'm 26, but I have double the years' work experience compared to my friends who went to uni – even if sometimes people in the industry aren't sure how seriously to take me because I look so much younger than they expect me to be at this stage in my career!'

He has clearly enjoyed the learning side of things too, completing a second Level 6 apprenticeship a few years ago.

'I really enjoy my job, and my new responsibilities as I manage whole projects and work directly with clients. I still don't have a grand plan for the future: just to keep going and see where it takes me.'

## EMPLOYER CASE STUDY: HENRY BOOT

Henry Boot PLC is a group of companies that create sustainable value and long-term growth from land, property and development and construction. Its head office is in Sheffield and the group employs circa 500 people, with offices all over the UK. It has a 137-year heritage with a proud history of working on key UK construction projects and now operates across the whole property value chain, acquiring land without planning permission, obtaining planning permission, developing sites and maintaining an investment portfolio. The company is still part owned by the Boot family, and as such has a family culture and recognises the value of its people in delivering its success.

They currently have 20 apprentices on a range of programmes from Level 2 up to Level 7, relating to a wide range of occupations. On the operational side, Henry Boot use Construction Management programmes at levels 4–6; for its Construction Plant sector it uses the Hire Controller Plant, Tools and Equipment programme. It also uses degree apprenticeships in Chartered Surveying and, for the support functions, apprenticeships at levels 4–7 in Marketing, HR, Finance, IT and Legal. The company is always seeking to utilise new, relevant apprenticeship programmes that become available, such as the level 7 Solicitor apprenticeship that an employee will be starting in 2023.

The company is committed to apprenticeships to provide opportunities for school leavers to enter the industry, as well as developing their existing employees. Craig Brown, Learning and Development Advisor for the Group says, 'The construction industry in particular has a well-documented skills shortage and apprenticeships are strategically essential for us to develop the skills and talent that we need for the future. EDI (Equality, Diversity & Inclusion) is very important to us, and we are able to promote apprenticeship vacancies through related initiatives. They are also a great mechanism to offer development opportunities to our existing staff, so that they can continue to develop valuable skills throughout their careers.'

Craig also highlights the effectiveness of apprenticeships for structured career progression: 'For most of our apprenticeship roles, apprentices can progress through the levels, often we can take an apprentice from Level 3 all the way through to degree or masters level, whilst accruing work experience along the way.'

Apprenticeships are becoming increasingly popular, and certain degree apprenticeships can attract large numbers of applications; but work still needs to be done on lesser-known apprenticeships and 'hidden industry roles' that potential apprentices, parents and school careers advisors may not know much about. Henry Boot recognises that there are fantastic opportunities available which may not be well-known, and the company has a strategic approach to school and community engagement to raise awareness of these opportunities.

They are conscious that it takes more than just enthusiasm to get apprenticeships right, as there are some challenges to the way apprenticeships are delivered in the UK. A company needs well-equipped line managers and mentors, as well as the capacity to be able to support apprenticeship programmes, and the provision and availability of good quality local training from colleges and universities.

For those looking to find an apprenticeship, Craig's message is: 'An apprenticeship is a fantastic entry point into a career. More routes into industry via apprenticeships are being developed year on year and are a great way to gain experience and qualifications whilst earning at the same time. When we recruit apprentices, we tend to ask about their strengths and interests, and look for enthusiasm and a willingness to learn, more so than their experience or academic achievement, so if you didn't quite get the grades you were expecting in school, don't worry, there are many opportunities out there for you.'

# Section 3
# What an apprenticeship entails

# Introduction to Section 3:
# What an apprenticeship entails

By now you should be clear that lots of people think apprenticeships are a good thing, most importantly young people themselves.

We will now look in more detail at how an apprenticeship works, what the various bits of terminology mean, who is involved and what some of the things to watch out for are.

Here is what we will look at.

- Apprenticeships are jobs.
- What an apprenticeship programme is.
- How an apprenticeship works.
- How you get the qualification (End Point Assessment).
- Different apprenticeship levels.
- English and maths requirements (often referred to as functional skills).
- The different organisations involved.
- Who pays for it and the financial implications.
- Things to watch out for.

# 3.1 An apprenticeship is a job

It is essential that you understand one thing more than anything else: an apprenticeship is a job.

It is not a 'place' on a programme or in a scheme. It is a real, live job that an employer pays your wages for with their own money. They – and only they – get to decide, first, whether a job exists within their organisation, and they – and only they – get to decide who gets that job and whether they stay in it (no training provider, no college or even the government can make an employer employ someone).

So what is a 'job'?

We use the word all the time but we rarely think more deeply about it. It is important that you do think about it, because it is the foundation of your apprenticeship and your career success.

Here are some of the answers I have often heard when asking young people embarking on an apprenticeship, 'What is a job?'

- 'It's a way to earn a living.'
- 'It's how you achieve your aspirations.'
- 'It's somewhere to express yourself.'
- 'It's where you contribute to society.'
- 'It's how you can apply your skills and knowledge.'

None of these answers are wrong, but they do not capture the crucial aspect of what a job is (and therefore of what an apprenticeship is).

A job is foremost a transaction, an exchange – your give your time, effort and skills to your employer and, in return, your employer gives you money.

This is fundamentally different from being at school, college or university: they get paid for you to be there, they exist to serve people like you. If people stopped attending their courses, they would cease to exist. They need you (or people like you).

An employer, by contrast does not need to employ you in order to exist. They have no obligation to create jobs – indeed, most employers try to keep the number of jobs they have to a minimum, because employing people is one of their main costs. They only choose to employ you for a basic reason: because they want you to do something for them, in return for which they will pay you a salary.

And this is the fundamental difference between an apprenticeship and going to university: in an apprenticeship, you get paid in return for doing something (while learning); at university, you pay and in return you get learning (perhaps while doing something).

# 3.2 What an apprenticeship programme is

An apprenticeship is a job in which the employer, with the support of an approved specialist apprenticeship training provider, employs a person – like you – and commits to train and develop them through a structured programme. In this way, the apprentice can obtain the knowledge, skills and behaviours required to be fully competent in the chosen occupation – and can demonstrate that they have done so.

Each apprenticeship programme has to be specific to a certain occupation (such as 'plumbing and domestic heating technician', 'data analyst' or 'engineering operative'). There are over 600 different apprenticeship programmes available at the time of writing (summer 2023). The official name of an approved apprenticeship programme is an 'Apprenticeship Standard' (they used to be called 'Frameworks' and there are still some of these older model apprenticeships available).

Each Apprenticeship Standard describes, in a handful of pages the duties typically required of that role, and for each duty the knowledge, skills and behaviours (KSBs as they are often referred to), that someone needs to be able to demonstrate at the end of their apprenticeship for them to become qualified in that occupation.

The Standard also defines how the person on the apprenticeship programme will be assessed as competent and qualified – the End Point Assessment; as well as providing the underpinning description of what the role is all about – the Occupational Standard.

The format of Standards sometimes varies, depending on what the guidance and rules were at the time the Standard was first developed.

New Apprenticeship Standards are continually being created and old ones phased out, as the economy evolves and employer requirements develop. For example, 'Artificial Intelligence data specialist' only came into existence as an apprenticeship in 2020.

A Standard can only exist if at least ten employers have voluntarily come together to create it, working with the Institute for Apprenticeships & Technical Education (IfATE, a government body) to make sure it is a robust programme. For many Standards, employers who normally compete hard against each other have collaborated to create apprenticeship programmes because they see how valuable it will be to them and their sector as a whole.

This means that if an Apprenticeship Standard exists, it represents a real demand in the real economy for these skills, and is a robust qualification.

# 3.3 How an apprenticeship works

The experience of doing a real job combined with a rich blend of different ways of learning will give you the knowledge, the skills and the behaviours you need to show that you are truly and fully competent in your chosen occupation. Boil it down and it's a common-sense way to learn how to do anything new.

How you will learn and practise will vary from employer to employer and from training provider to training provider, as they will all have different ways of doing things. Your line manager will be crucial to your experience – if they are committed to you achieving your Standard, you should be fine.

Key elements of your learning are likely to include the following.

- Learning 'on the job': watching others work and copying them, being supervised as you try these tasks out for the first time, getting detailed feedback on what you did well and what you could do better. This is how the majority of your learning will happen – it will be amazingly practical.

- Learning 'off the job': this is the bit that is most like 'classroom' learning, whether it is in-person or online; you will work through study materials, either on your own or in a peer group. This is where you will learn new concepts and knowledge (the theory), and in some cases you will have the chance to try out and practise new skills and techniques away from your actual work. You might get to work on team exercises too. Some of this will be delivered by your employer, but most will be delivered by your training provider.

- Coaching: if you are lucky, your line manager will be good at 'coaching', i.e. helping you figure out how to improve and learn for yourself, rather than just teaching or showing you directly. Your training provider will provide someone (sometimes called a Skills Coach or Advisor) to support and guide you through your apprenticeship to successful completion; they will make sure you get all the associated paperwork done too.

- Mentoring: some employers will link you up with someone else in the organisation to be your mentor. Typically, this person will not be directly involved in your day-to-day work, meaning that they can be more impartial, and can help you to 'step back' to see the bigger picture, as well as share with you the insights and wisdom they may have accumulated during their career.

- Your own extra learning: often your employer or training provider will give you the opportunity to do extra study by yourself, and some employers may also make extra learning resources available for you.

It is this combination of different ways of learning that makes apprenticeship learning special. As you progress through your apprenticeship, you should find yourself getting better and better at your job, and learning more and more as you go. You can try out different ways of doing things to find what approach works best for you, with people around you who want to help you learn and succeed. All the way you will be guided to a successful outcome – as long as you put in the hard work!

# 3.4 How you pass an apprenticeship and become qualified

An important part of an apprenticeship is that at the end you get an official Government authorised (and legally protected) qualification that is increasingly recognised by employers and society as the benchmark for proving that you have successfully begun your chosen career.

*A quick note: The rest of this chapter applies to England only. Apprenticeship programmes in Scotland, Wales and Northern Ireland have slightly different systems for achieving the apprenticeship qualification. You can find out more at:*

- *apprenticeships.scot (Scotland)*
- *careerswales.gov.wales/apprenticeship-search (Wales)*
- *nidirect.gov.uk/services/search-apprenticeship-opportunities (Northern Ireland).*

To get this you need to go through a process called End Point Assessment, or EPA for short.

It is conducted by an independent assessor based in a special End Point Assessment Organisation (EPAO), so it is robust and objective, just like any other public exam such as GCSEs or A levels.

The format for an EPA depends on the particular Standard (details are available on the IfATE website as part of each Standard), but will include things like:

- a review of an evidence portfolio that you have built up through your apprenticeship
- a structured conversation about your experiences
- a project in 'closed conditions' for half a day.

You may not like the thought of having to do a 'test' at the end – indeed, one of the motivations for doing an apprenticeship is to avoid academic exams. Many people worry about the EPA, and worries about it are a major reason why some people do not complete their apprenticeship.

But you should not worry: think of the EPA as the moment when your hard work and achievements over the last year or more get properly recognised. Your independent assessor is not looking for you to be a brilliant presenter or to be 'clever', they are looking only for the evidence that you have the knowledge, skills and behaviours that are required in your Standard. And the good news is, your employer and training provider will only put you forward for the EPA if they think you already have that evidence.

It is important to ask early and often about what is expected of you for End Point Assessment, right from the moment you first apply, and again when you start your apprenticeship: if you know what is expected of you and when, you are more likely to succeed and less likely to worry about it. Just ask – and ask again!

If you have done the apprenticeship job to the best of your ability, engaged with all the learning opportunities you have had and prepared properly, then you have nothing to fear from the EPA.

For many of the Standards, if you do really well it is possible to be awarded a Merit or a Distinction – so something for you to really aim for.

# 3.5 What are all the different apprenticeship 'levels'?

Pick up most 'official' guidance on apprenticeships and quite soon you'll be reading about levels, starting at Level 2 and going up to Level 7.

What are these levels, are they important and why do they get so much attention?

Levels are a way for the education and skills sector to know that they are comparing 'like with like' between different courses, regardless of whether they are academic or vocational or a hybrid. Roughly speaking, the level describes how hard the qualification is and/or what level of knowledge and expertise is required. For example, you have to know more about biology to get a degree (Level 6) in Biology than you do to have to get Biology GCSE (Level 2).

In academic qualifications, GCSEs are Level 2 qualifications, A levels are Level 3, and an undergraduate degree is Level 6.

If you are doing a non-academic qualification, such as an HND or an apprenticeship, the same system is used. For example, an HNC (Higher National Certificate) is Level 4, a Higher National Diploma is Level 5 and so on.

The lowest level of an apprenticeship is Level 2 (there are no Level 1 apprenticeships) and the highest level is Level 7 (there is no Level 8 apprenticeship – in academic studies, Level 8 is a PhD).

Roughly speaking, the table on the following page shows how you can usefully think about the different levels.

## Apprenticeship levels

| Level | Often called... | Equivalent to | You might consider this level if you... |
|---|---|---|---|
| 2 | Intermediary apprenticeship | GCSEs | • have GCSEs but not A levels<br>• want an entry level role to test out, which you can build from if you find you like it.<br>*Typically lasts a year, perhaps a bit more.* |
| 3 | Advanced apprenticeship | A levels/Level 3 BTECs/T Levels | • have done your A levels<br>• want to start a career that will be new to you<br>• want to try something out before committing to it<br>• have left school at 16 but already have a particular aptitude for a particular field and certainty that you want to work in it.<br>*Typically lasts between a year and 18 months.* |
| 4 | Higher apprenticeship | HNC/Certificate of Higher Education | • have already done a relevant Level 3 apprenticeship<br>• have done your A levels and the higher apprenticeship is in an area where you already have proven aptitude (perhaps through a combination of academic work, work experience and/or an in-depth hobby).<br>*Typically lasts 18–24 months.* |
| 5 | Higher apprenticeship | HND/Diploma of Higher Education/ Foundation Degree | • want to qualify in an occupation above entry level but which does not require a degree<br>*Typically lasts two years.* |
| 6 | Degree apprenticeship | Degree | • are committed to an occupation<br>• have work experience already<br>• have just done your A levels<br>• want to get a degree while doing an apprenticeship.<br>*It takes three years or more.* |
| 7 | Higher degree/ professional apprenticeship | Masters | • want to go even further than a degree apprenticeship<br>• want to receive 'chartered' status or other official recognition that you are now a fully-fledged member of the profession<br>• are mid-career, and are looking for a way of training for a step up in your career.<br>*Typically lasts 12–18 months.* |

It is common for people to do just one apprenticeship, at the level required to become qualified for that particular occupation, e.g. Level 3 for a bricklayer, Level 4 for a data analyst or Level 6 for a nurse. However, it is also possible to do multiple apprenticeships, as several of the apprentice case studies in this book have done, moving up levels over time. You might use an 'entry' level apprenticeship (e.g. at Level 2 or 3) to get into the occupation and test whether it is right for you; if it is, then you can progress into a related apprenticeship at a higher level and so on. You might even shift between different occupational areas as you move up.

Often doing the Level 6 and 7 apprenticeships enable you to obtain full professional status, e.g. you can become a fully qualified accountant, lawyer or doctor. These are roles that previously you had to have achieved a university degree and further qualifications to enter the profession.

Have a look at the Institute of Apprenticeships occupational maps (instituteforapprenticeships.org/occupational-maps) to find out more about how different levels of apprenticeships fit together.

## 💡 Interesting idea: Degree apprenticeships

Degree apprenticeships were introduced in 2015 alongside other significant reforms of apprenticeships, all of which were designed to improve the quality and reputation of apprenticeships overall. Degree apprenticeships embody the 'parity of esteem' between apprenticeships and degrees. Since then, over 150,000 people have started a degree apprenticeship in the UK, with numbers increasing every year.

A degree apprenticeship combines an apprenticeship with a degree, by using a university degree award as part of the off-the-job learning component of the apprenticeship. The person undertaking the apprenticeship is expected to do as much work for their employer as any other apprentice does in their apprenticeship. As well as undertaking the EPA at the end of the programme, the apprentice also undertakes the assessments associated with getting a degree as well.

'Degrees from United Kingdom Higher Education Institutions (HEI) have a particularly strong reputation globally, and are seen as "the gold standard". Their combination with apprenticeships is therefore hugely powerful.' So says Daniel Lally, who is responsible for all the degree apprenticeship programmes at Sheffield Hallam University, a leading university provider of degree apprenticeships.

Degree apprenticeships last at least as long as the degree they are associated with, so typically 3 years (although Masters degree apprenticeships may be less than this, and some may be up to six years long).

While this all seems like quite a lot of work to sustain over a longer period of time than for many apprenticeships, there are two major benefits to doing a degree apprenticeship.

1. Unlike with a 'normal' apprenticeship, you get a degree as well as an apprenticeship qualification, without paying for it or having to borrow – the university tuition fees are covered by the apprenticeship system (see below for more on how apprenticeships are funded).

2. Unlike a 'normal' degree, you get to apply what you are learning academically in your degree directly into the real world, making the learning much more powerful.

Degree apprenticeships are growing steadily, with nearly 20,000 people aged 16-23 starting one in the year 2021/22 (while another 23,000 people over the age of 24 also started one).

The reasons for going for a degree apprenticeship include the following.

- To get a degree without having to incur debt and while earning a salary.

- You are fairly certain about both the career you want to go into and, ideally, the employer you want to start your career with (because it is commonly a commitment of at least three years).

- You want to get a degree but also see the value of doing an apprenticeship (particularly getting work experience).

It is worth noting that a degree apprenticeship is a pretty full-on option when it comes to time, both in terms of time commitment (for multiple years) and managing your time between work, study and other obligations. Some of them also require a level of personal experience and maturity that not everyone will have when they are leaving school.

# 3.6 English and maths, aka functional skills

*A quick note: This chapter applies to apprenticeships in England only. Apprenticeship programmes in Scotland, Wales and Northern Ireland have slightly different systems for functional skills.*

The Government (at the time of writing) requires that anyone achieving an apprenticeship has to demonstrate a minimum skill level in English and maths. These are sometimes referred to as 'functional skills' (because you need them to 'function' in the world of work).

The intention here is straightforward: the Government wants more people to have better English and maths skills, and believe it is important for the reputation of apprenticeships that anyone getting one has achieved a reasonable level in them.

For a Level 2 apprenticeship, the level required for English and Maths is Level 1 (a GCSE at grades 1-3 or equivalent), for a Level 3 apprenticeship or higher, the level required is typically Level 2 (equivalent to a 4 or above in GCSE), although this may vary according to the requirements of the employer (or sometimes the training provider).

This seems pretty simple and reasonable. In practice, however, it can cause quite a lot of irritation and stress in the apprenticeship system, as it is often seen as unnecessary by employers, training providers and apprentices themselves. Why should someone doing a job that does not require much formal maths or formal English techniques have to show that they can use them? After all, part of the value of an apprenticeship is that it is practical: it shouldn't have to have any academic elements.

As such, there is an ongoing debate around functional skills, and the Government has made some changes recently to relax the requirements, and it is possible it will make more changes in the future.

The key thing for you, as an apprentice, is to understand as early as possible what you need to do to get to the level required in order to complete your apprenticeship. Ask your training provider and employer early. Do not let fears about functional skills put you off from doing an apprenticeship; it is an administrative faff at worst, and for some people it's a good opportunity to brush up on skills that they struggled with at school.

# 3.7 Who are all the different organisations involved?

*A quick note: This chapter applies to apprenticeships in England only. Apprenticeship programmes in Scotland, Wales and Northern Ireland have slightly different systems and therefore there are different organisations involved, albeit all looking to achieve the same overall outcomes.*

Lots of different organisations will be involved in your apprenticeship.

- Your employer: without an organisation to employ you, there are no jobs, without jobs there are no apprenticeships. So employers are **the** critical organisation for your apprenticeship. Their obligation is to provide you with a proper job, good line management and the opportunities to learn and practise all elements of the apprenticeship. They can also help you to get the best out of your training provider and help prepare you for the EPA.

- Training providers: it is a Government requirement that every apprenticeship is delivered by an approved apprenticeship training provider, registered on the official Apprenticeship Providers and Assessment Register (APAR). There are three sorts of training providers: 1) local colleges 2) independent training providers (either companies or non-for-profit organisations) and 3) some large employers are also their own training providers. Training providers are obliged to give you what you need to pass your apprenticeship and to look out for your safety and wellbeing. They ensure that you are systematically covering all the Knowledge, Skills and Behaviours set out in the Apprenticeship Standard. They can also help with your relationship with your employer.

- End Point Assessment Organisation: more commonly referred to as the EPAO, they are independent from both your employer and your training provider. They will run your EPA and decide your result. They also have to be registered on the APAR.

- The Government: there are three parts of Government that you might need to know about (but you could go through your whole apprenticeship without ever coming into contact with them).

  ◆ The Institute for Apprenticeships & Technical Education (IfATE) is the part of Government that has responsibility for Apprenticeship Standards and T levels (qualifications that focus on vocational skills). It oversees and approves what apprenticeships are available and determines the maximum funding a provider can receive for delivering it. It runs the process through which employers can collaborate to create new apprenticeships. Since 2018, IfATE has overseen the creation of over 600 different apprenticeships, with each and every one led by at least ten employers (and sometimes many more).

  ◆ The Education and Skills Funding Agency (ESFA) is part of the Department of Education and is responsible for making sure the apprenticeship system as a whole works. While the elected politicians who are Education ministers make decisions about what they want, it is the ESFA who put it into action, making sure the system is working and keeping track of progress. They register training providers and make sure the providers keep records and claim funding only where they are supposed to.

  ◆ You may well have heard of OFSTED, because it is the organisation that also inspects schools and colleges. Every apprenticeships training provider will be inspected at some point by OFSTED. Most will be inspected every five or six years, but if there are concerns they may be inspected more often.

There are four 'grades' that OFSTED give an organisation:

- outstanding
- good
- requires improvement
- inadequate.

Chapter 6.4 talks about how you might use these grades to judge whether a training provider is right for you.

# 3.8 Who pays for your apprenticeship and what are the financial implications?

Not you! And that's a seriously important benefit for you of doing an apprenticeship.

*A quick note: This chapter applies to apprenticeships in England only. Apprenticeship programmes in Scotland, Wales and Northern Ireland have slightly different systems – although they are all free for apprentices to participate in.*

If your employer has a paybill of £3 million or more a year, then it will pay something called the Apprenticeship Levy. This is an additional tax of 0.5% that they can only spend on apprenticeship training fees (paid to the training provider) – if they don't use it for apprenticeships, then they lose it to the taxman. If they are smaller than that and do not pay the levy, then the Government pays 95% of the training provider fees, with the employer paying the other 5% themselves. If the firm is really small (fewer than 50 employees) and the apprentice is 18 or younger when they start then the Government will pay 100% of the fees.

The good news, as far as you're concerned, is that you don't need to worry about any of this. Employers will typically be pretty positive about spending on your apprenticeship: either they pay the Apprenticeship Levy and will be pleased to be 'using up' their levy (instead of it going to the taxman) or they are a small firm getting a huge subsidy from the Government.

**You do not have to pay any fees, either upfront or through borrowing – there is no debt.**

There is additional financial support available from the Government for young people who, for whatever reason, have been living in care, which goes directly to the young person. (In addition, the Government provides extra funding to both the employer and the training provider to help with any extra costs, incentivising them to go the extra mile to recruit care leavers).

Crucially, you earn a salary while you are an apprentice – after all, you are doing a real job. Your salary is paid for by your employer, out of their own money. This is a significant outlay and investment in your skills and time. As such, you must always be vigilant that you are doing your very best to justify your employer's faith in you.

The apprenticeship minimum wage (at the time of writing, summer 2023) is £5.28 an hour, which for a typical 37.5-hour week contract equates to a £10,296 annual salary. Many apprenticeships pay more than this, and some quite a lot more, often at a level similar to that of graduate programmes. There is no definitive data on what apprentices earn on average, though there are some sources that give a good indication of what you could get; according to Totaljobs (totaljobs.com) the average apprenticeship wage is £20,536 per annum, according to Glassdoor (glassdoor.co.uk) it is £19,835 per annum and the website findapprenticeships.co.uk says that salaries for apprentices range between £15,000 and £30,000 per year. Many employers also give their apprentices pay rises while they are doing their apprenticeship.

Remember: if you earn more than £12,570 a year, you will be earning enough to have to pay tax – that means that not every pound of your salary will come to you. You can ask your employer what your 'net' pay will be (your total pay less your taxes) to find out what you will actually get each month.

There is not much up-to-date research on longer term wage outcomes for people who have done apprenticeships. However, in 2016 the then Minister for Skills, Nick Boles, told the House of Commons: 'Apprenticeships have excellent wage returns for individuals over their working life. These add up to between £48,000 and £74,000 for Level 2 apprenticeships and between £77,000 and £117,000 for Level 3 apprentices. Those completing an apprenticeship at Level 4 or above could earn £150,000 more on average over their lifetime.'

This is backed up by a 2018 technical study from the London School of Economics (LSE) that there are grounds for 'optimism that apprenticeships really do generate a positive return in the labour market for young people'. This study also highlights the significant and wide variation in outcomes depending on the apprenticeship and the employer.

Nowadays, most wages are paid monthly rather than weekly, which makes things administratively simple for your employer, but means you have to wait a whole month to receive the money into your bank account. You need to consider whether this could be a problem for your first month of work, when you may have outgoings before you get your first pay cheque.

It is also important to think through the impact on your household if other people in it receive benefits of any kind. This is because benefit payments are often calculated on the basis of the income of everyone in the household. So if you start earning money, others in your household may find their benefits being reduced. But this is not always the case: you should definitely check with a training provider, a local Jobcentre Plus or a local Citizens Advice office.

Finally, you need to factor in the costs of going to work that you will have to cover from your salary, such as getting to and from work and lunch (although some employers may provide financial support for this too, or in the case of lunch, provide it). If you are required to wear a particular company uniform or particular clothing to do the job, then the company should provide that for you. But for an office job where you just want to look the part, then you will need to buy that yourself. Lots of employers are willing to provide short-term loans to help you get your first season ticket or indeed your first work clothes until you get your first pay slip, so do ask if you think this could be a problem.

# 3.9 Things to watch out for

Apprenticeships are a great option, and one that is increasingly recognised in the UK and around the world. However, to help you make the right choice for you it is important to understand some of the pitfalls as well.

There are four things in particular to watch out for.

1. Not every apprenticeship is amazing.
2. The process of getting an apprenticeship can seem bewildering.
3. Apprenticeships are hard work.
4. Many parents and teachers still don't get it.

## 1. Not every apprenticeship is amazing

There are many truly amazing apprenticeships. Just reading the case studies in this guidebook or elsewhere online and you will see evidence for the life-changing power of apprenticeships, as they enable people to find and flourish in careers, often beyond their wildest dreams. Take a look at amazingapprenticeships.com or the National Apprenticeship Service website (https://engage.apprenticeships.gov.uk/aan-testimonials).

But this is not true for every apprenticeship. Government figures show that in the year 2021/22 around 40% of people who started an apprenticeship did not finish it. While sometimes they do not finish for good reasons – e.g. they get promoted or move somewhere else in the country – often it is because the apprenticeship does not meet their expectations.

Recent research by The St Martin's Group (a group of employers and training providers committed to enhancing and growing apprenticeships across the economy) showed that some apprentices do not get the support and advice they need from either their employer or their training provider (or both) and end up dropping out.

The reasons cited for a poor experience include:

- the apprenticeship being poorly organised
- too high a workload
- poor quality teaching
- lack of support from the employer and/or the training provider
- a more general loss of motivation or interest.

The research discovered that the apprentices most likely to drop out are those doing a Level 6 or 7 programme, those working for 'micro' employers, those aged over 50 and those with a disability or health condition.

The EPA seems to be a specific source of tension and worry for some apprentices: what it will be like, whether they will be able to prepare themselves for it, whether they will get support from their employer and training provider in time and, in general, how stressful it will be. The less an apprentice knows about and is confident about their EPA the less likely they are to successfully complete their apprenticeship. There is also some evidence that some apprentices, having successfully got into their career via the apprenticeship, do not feel the need to actually complete it, do the EPA and get the qualification.

The two main organisations involved in your apprenticeship are your employer and your training provider. How committed and capable they are to supporting you is key: you must research both thoroughly in order to give yourself the best chance of your apprenticeship being successful. Chapter 6.4 has specific guidance on how to find out if a potential employer or training provider is good.

By the way, this is a reflection of the economy as a whole: some employers are great employers, some are not; some training organisations are brilliant, some are not. And, of course, there is a whole spectrum in between. It is not surprising that apprenticeships on offer are also of varied quality.

However, the most important person in determining whether an apprenticeship is successful or not is you. That is why doing some hard thinking about yourself, about what you want out of a career and about what you enjoy is so crucial, which is what Sections 5 and 6 of this book are all about.

## 2. The application process can seem bewildering

There are over 1 million employers in the UK. All of them (potentially) could be offering apprenticeships.

They are not spread evenly across the country: some apprenticeships are only available in certain locations.

Nor is there a set timetable for them to recruit – the economy doesn't work on a neat yearly cycle – so they could be recruiting at any time of the year.

There is no guarantee that there will be the apprenticeships being advertised that you want to do when you want to do them or where you want to do them.

Employers are all unique, with their own unique  pressures and ambitions, as well as unique personalities and dynamics. It is not surprising that no two recruitment processes are the same, with each one having different processes, timetables and expectations.

Employers are often looking for slightly different things: attributes that make you a great candidate for one apprenticeship may not matter at all for another one, and the thing that rules you out of one opportunity may be the very thing that gets you another.

UCAS has begun incorporating apprenticeships alongside university places in the application process for post-school education and training. This is really welcome and shows just how much the educational 'establishment' now understands and values apprenticeships. It should make it easier to find and do the initial application for apprenticeships. However, employers will still want their own, individual recruitment process in addition to whatever process UCAS offers.

The upshot is that applying for apprenticeships will remain more cumbersome than applying for university. But that's because you are stepping into the real economy (with all its inherent complications and messiness), rather than staying in the world of education (which by contrast is relatively simple and straightforward).

Finding an apprenticeship takes more research, more effort and more time than finding a place at university. You need to factor this into your planning, and not be surprised that getting an apprenticeship is not as straightforward as getting a place at uni.

For advice and guidance on evaluating your options and making the process of applying for apprenticeships manageable, see Sections 6 and 7.

## 3. Apprenticeships are hard work

Apprenticeships are not an easy option. Because it is a job **and** learning that leads to a qualification, it means that you need to do a lot. You need to be able to switch between 'job' and 'learning' modes quickly while integrating 'the doing' and 'the learning'.

If the apprenticeship is your first job in your new career it may feel like it is a high-pressure situation – more than any casual job you might have done before. You want to get it right.

At the same time as you are learning how to do the nuts and bolts of your job well, you are also learning about the 'rules' of your new workplace. Those rules are sometimes explicit (those are the easy ones to learn!), but there are also the implicit unspoken 'rules'. Figuring out what these are – even when people are kind and helpful – can be difficult and stressful.

You will meet lots of new people of all different ages and from many different backgrounds. You may have direct contact with customers, who are unlikely to care that you are an apprentice and just starting out – they will still want their needs to be met!

Figuring out how to get on with new people, alongside doing the nuts and bolts of your job and keeping on top of your studies, takes a lot of energy and time management.

## 4. Many parents & teachers don't get apprenticeships

Some parents and some teachers do get what an apprenticeship is. For example, a recent report by PwC found that a growing number of middle-class parents have cottoned on to the benefits of apprenticeships. But many still do not understand apprenticeships, and believe that university remains the 'right' route for their children.

The same is true of many teachers, who are working from outdated statistics about the 'value' of a degree for employment prospects or are looking back to their own experience.

The implication of this for you is that if you want to go down the apprenticeship route you may find yourself having to justify and explain yourself far more than if you go for a more 'traditional' route. You may well come under pressure to go down the 'uni' option, and you will need to steel yourself to explain your choice (again and again!).

While this may not seem like a reason to be cautious about the apprenticeship route, you should not underestimate the headwinds that could blow against your choice.

Chapters 4.3 and 4.4 can help you understand what's behind people's pro-university bias and help you manage it.

The good news about all of these potential downsides is that you can do something about them.

- *Not every apprenticeship is amazing* – so make sure you understand yourself well and do your research effectively into the apprenticeship options out there in order to maximise the chances of finding an apprenticeship that will be amazing for you.
- *The process of getting an apprenticeship can seem bewildering* – but, with the help of this book and others advising and guiding you, you can figure out, step by step, which apprenticeships to apply for, how to go about applying for them, thus minimising the stress while maximising your chances of success.
- *Apprenticeships are hard work* – but if you know this, you can be prepared for it and, indeed, you might even be motivated by it. If you are able to find yourself an apprenticeship that works for you, then the hard work will be part of the reward.
- *Many parents and teachers still don't get what an apprenticeship is* – so equip yourself with the information and arguments necessary to have sensible and productive conversations with your parents and teachers about why you are considering an apprenticeship.

# Section 3 summary:
# What an apprenticeship entails

An apprenticeship is a job – a transaction between the apprentice and their employer; it is not a 'place' on a programme provided for the benefit of the apprentice.

It is defined by a 'Standard', created by employers and approved by IfATE (part of Government), that sets out the knowledge, skills and behaviours (KSBs) required to become qualified in the named occupation. The learning happens on and off the job, through coaching and mentoring and under the apprentice's own steam – a powerful blend of learning inputs.

To pass the apprenticeship and become qualified, every apprentice has to go through an End Point Assessment (EPA), an independent assessment involving different forms of evidence, but all related to the apprentice's demonstrated ability to do the job they have been doing.

Apprenticeships, like all qualifications in the UK, come at specified levels (from 2 to 7) that indicate how stretching and advanced the apprenticeship is. That means there are apprenticeships available, regardless of your current starting point, that can take you all the way up to professional status in prestigious professions.

Apprenticeships also require apprentices to achieve a certain level of English and maths. Although exactly what this requires is adjusted frequently by Government, you can take the sting out of it by working closely and early with your training provider.

There are a number of different organisations involved: the employer, the training provider, the End Point Assessment Organisation. In the background are also IfATE, the Education and Skills Funding Agency and OFSTED.

A huge attraction of an apprenticeship is that it costs the apprentice nothing – indeed, they get to earn a salary as they go through the apprenticeship (the minimum is just over £10,000 per year, but many apprentices earn much more). Lifetime earnings outcomes are good for people who have completed an apprenticeship.

But there are things to watch out for too.

- Not every apprenticeship is amazing.
- The process of getting an apprenticeship can seem bewildering.
- Apprenticeships are hard work.
- Many parents and teachers still don't get it.

The good news is there are tried and tested ways to manage each one of these potential downsides.

## APPRENTICE CASE STUDY: CHRIS SMITH

When Chris finished his GCSEs he knew he did not want to follow in the footsteps of many people he knew, working in the gig economy or in factory jobs where there was uncertainty and little possibility of growth and development.

At the time, he also thought he knew what he did want: a job in sports management and leadership. He spent two years studying various courses at college, undertaking placements and entry-level jobs, only to discover that the career he had assumed might exist in fact did not. 'At the time it felt like I had completely wasted two years. I thought I knew what my dream career was, but it turns out the jobs to make it happen just weren't there.'

In order to keep himself busy and get a bit of money he started doing gardening odd jobs for family and friends. Before he knew it he was getting recommendations and finding that he really enjoyed it. It felt like a natural and sensible next step to start looking for a more formal job and career in the same line of work.

'An apprenticeship seemed like the best route by far for what I wanted: stability (because it is a proper job not a series of gig-economy jobs), the opportunity to learn and develop and, of course, a qualification too.' Chris was delighted to get a job in the Outdoor Spaces and Parks team in his local council, Halton Borough Council, in the north-west of England doing a Level 2 apprenticeship in Horticulture, Amenity and Landscaping.

He applied himself diligently and soon found himself developing a bit of a specialism in street furniture installation and maintenance: everything in a street that's not the road or pavement (benches, bollards, playgrounds, football pitches, fencing, etc.). It's something he has gone on to excel in. 'I really enjoy being good at something, and being recognised for it. I love the camaraderie of my team. I love being active and outdoors – strangely I prefer winter to summer! As someone who lives locally, I really like seeing things that I have installed being used and enjoyed by members of the public – it's really satisfying.'

The apprenticeship has played a key role in Chris's life: 'My team leaders really bought into the idea of me as an apprentice: they looked out for me, they supported me and they really helped me to understand the role and progress quickly.' More than that, it has helped shape him as a person: 'The apprenticeship gave me huge confidence. It's been phenomenal. It has made me a whole person.'

He has progressed far and fast, and is now the person responsible for one of the biggest parks in the whole borough. He is looking at his best next steps, which could include a move into management. He also has deep confidence because of the combination of his skills, his experience, his qualification and his belief that he can learn in whatever situation he finds himself, and that he will thrive wherever his career takes him.

As he says, 'I am my own parachute.'

💼 **EMPLOYER CASE STUDY: BT GROUP**

BT Group is not just one of the UK's largest and best-known companies, it is also one of the country's most significant employers of apprentices.

With a 60-year track record of employing and training apprentices, in the last five years alone nearly 14,000 people have completed an apprenticeship with BT Group across around 30 different occupations, ranging from the engineers who are installing fibre broadband to data analysts figuring out which customers are using which products, and how and why.

Apprentices have played a strategically important role for BT Group – and, for the rest of us. Tens of thousands of apprentices have been trained and employed as part of Openreach's full fibre rollout across the country – currently operating at connecting an average rate of 62,000 premises per week.

'Without our apprentices and the apprenticeship programmes through which they have been trained, we would not have been able to achieve what we have,' says BT Group's Head of Apprenticeships, Jamie Pemberton-Legg. 'Apprentices are not a "nice to have" for us at BT Group – they are an essential part of our skills and talent pipeline.'

And it works for the people doing the apprenticeships too: over 80% of those who have done their apprenticeships are still working for BT Group five years after they have qualified.

Jamie continues: 'Apprenticeships are a brilliant way to bring fresh talent into the business, and to support them through the business. They are productive, committed and loyal. Apprenticeships are also a really effective way for us to hire people from diverse backgrounds – we value the benefits that difference can bring, helping us to broaden and deepen our expertise, customer relationships and ultimately get us closer to our goal of sustainable growth.'

As the rapid pace of technology-driven change continues, BT Group knows that apprenticeships are going to continue to be a vital way to build and nurture the skills it needs for thousands of new job roles that are only now coming into existence.

The other option for an employer like BT Group is to go out to the open labour market to get the skilled people it needs – but this can be very expensive, and the company still has to invest in these already-experienced people, in order to train them in how to work at BT Group. Graduates are also an important part of how BT hires staff. Jamie points out that apprentices are proven to be committed, 'sticky' and keen to get practical on-the-job experience: 'My colleagues like that apprentices are so grounded, and extremely good in practical terms.'

In Jamie's experience, the people who are most likely to flourish in an apprenticeship are those who:

- know enough about a role to be able to fully commit to it for the duration of the apprenticeship (even if they ultimately decide to go down another career path)
- are proactive and ready and willing to share their fresh thinking
- can communicate confidently in a business context and are open to learn quickly what is professionally appropriate
- are willing to give things a go – even if they might not succeed at first.

Jamie also has really useful advice for people as they embark on an apprenticeship: 'As you start your apprenticeship, look around you to figure out how things work – observe what "normal" is. Remember that your line manager may be from a different generation and have a different way of communicating. Always ask questions, even if it feels a bit awkward – you will always be glad that you have. If you are struggling (with anything), don't be afraid to speak up either to your employer or your training provider – they are there to help you after all. And lean on your peers as well – peer-to-peer networks are vital (and you can give back as well as receive): the Association of Apprentices is really good for this.'

# Section 4
# What you need to know about university and other options

# Introduction to Section 4: What you need to know about university and other options

It is almost certain that you will have been told about going to university while at school. If you have been half-way successful in your academic studies it is very likely that you will have been encouraged to 'go to uni'.

Sometimes, the advice is so overwhelming and ubiquitous, you could be forgiven for thinking that university is the only option for you once you have finished school.

It is also straightforward to apply for university: the UCAS form means just one application process to five universities out of 160. That application continues to work for you, via the 'clearing' process, even if you do not get the grades you hoped for. In addition, universities are big enough and (normally) well organised enough to put on engaging and appealing open days where they treat you like a VIP.

In parts of our culture, 'going to uni' is seen as an expected rite of passage. And for some communities, going to university is seen as even more important than that: it is seen as a sign of belonging and acceptance here in the UK.

This emphasis on 'going to uni' is reflected in the numbers: according to the House of Commons Library, there were 2.86 million people in total studying at university in the UK in 2022 – nearly 4% of the entire population. Over 750,000 applied for university courses in 2022 of whom 560,000 started – 45% of 18-year-olds applied for a university place.

While university can be a good option in the right circumstances, its benefits are by no means guaranteed and it is an expensive option, whether you (or your family) are paying upfront or with money borrowed through a Student Loan.

It is really important, therefore, that you step back and really think about what the university option is in order to know whether it is right for you.

There are many detailed guidebooks on applying to university, and this section does not aim to replicate them – if uni is an attractive option to you, you should definitely look at them and take detailed advice.

This section will cover the following.

- What the benefits of going to university are.
- The reasons to think twice.
- An explanation of pro-university bias.
- Some advice on how to handle pro-university bias.
- An introduction to your other main options and their pros and cons.

# 4.1 The reasons to go to university

There are five main reasons to go to university.

1. To study a subject you love.
2. To help secure a good career.
3. To have fun.
4. To learn and grow as a person.
5. To have the time and space to figure out what you want to do next.

## 1. To study a subject you love

If you do a course where you are interested in the subject matter for its own sake, then three (or more) years studying can be a complete joy. This is especially true if you are learning from renowned experts with enthusiastic fellow learners.

You can find yourself made truly happy by what you are studying and learning. You can learn lots about yourself and the amazing world in which we live. You may even go on to become a researcher or academic in the subject you are studying – in which case your love of the subject as an undergraduate student will also lead you directly to your career.

## 2. To help secure a good career

For some people, going to university is a stepping stone to a great career. According to Higher Education Statistics Authority (HESA) research in 2019/20, 89% of graduates were employed or in further study 15 months after completing their degree. Overall, graduates have earned around 11% more over their lifetime than those without a degree.

There are typically three ways in which a university experience can help you get a good career.

i. You acquire valuable knowledge and learn useful skills (this is enhanced if the course and/or university has a strong reputation).
ii. A 'sandwich year' or industry placement as part of the course gives you a lift up into a career (only relevant to certain courses).

    **iii.** Extra-curricular activities enable you to practise and prove work-relevant skills.

## i. You acquire knowledge & learn skills

It is likely that some of what you learn at university, whether knowledge or skills, will be useful as you get on the career ladder. Clearly, the closer the link between what you study and your job, the more useful the degree will be to your career. But even if you do a degree in a subject that has little to do with what you end up doing there are likely to be transferable skills – such as research skills, critical thinking, presentation and organisational skills – that you hone through your studies and can then use in your career.

The positive impact of university learning on potential careers is enhanced if the course and/or the university that you attend has a good reputation. Every university, eager to have you apply for them, will make strong claims about this. It is important you do your own research and come to your own conclusions.

## ii. A 'sandwich year' or industry placement

A number of university courses include a 'year out' – normally the third year out of four – in which students work for a 'host' company in order to develop an understanding of how their academic studies relate to 'the real world'. Often the student is able to build a strong relationship with their host company and return to work for them full time after graduation. The placement year in these cases is undoubtedly a strong route into a future career.

## iii. Extra-curricular activities to build work skills

People often use the spare time that they have at university to get involved in activities and clubs where they organise things and work as a team. This could be sports teams, hobbies or interest groups (from politics to ballroom dancing), or running entertainment events for fellow students. It is even possible to set up your own business while at university. Many students have part-time jobs, often in the hospitality industry, and others volunteer for charities.

As such, university students are able to learn and practise attributes and skills necessary for the world of work. These, as much as the content of their degree, are often what employers are impressed by during job applications.

## 3. To have fun

This is often a major draw for young people when thinking about whether to go to university: the stories about what people have done while they have been at university are often legendary! This could be the social life (lots of people do not want to miss out on the 'rite of passage' that is Freshers' Week), the opportunity to use the available spare time for activities and hobbies, or simply the opportunity to hang out in a non-pressured environment away from home with new friends.

This should not be underestimated, and is a genuine reason to go to university.

## 4. To learn & grow as a person

Moving away from home to live independently from your family for three years is a great way to discover yourself as a person and make the transition from being a school-age student to being an adult. If your home life has been difficult growing up, university can be a great stepping stone into a more positive adult life.

You are now in charge of your daily routine; you have to sort out your 'life logistics'; and you are independent (at least in term time) from the adults who have previously been around in your life. It can be a truly 'formative' period where you become yourself as an adult.

## 5. To have time & space to figure out what to do next

If you have left school uncertain about what you should do next, then university provides a tried and tested way for you to take the time, while continuing to develop yourself and learn, to figure out what you might want to do.

It helps to have a couple of years in which you can observe people in the year or two above you as they go through the process of working out what to do and applying for jobs. And, of course, you will have employers coming to your university to promote their careers to you and a careers department to advise you.

As you learn, as you become more independent and as you become more self-aware, you may well find yourself in a much better position aged 21 or 22, at the end of your degree, than you are at age 18 to have a good idea about what you might want to do next.

# 4.2 The reasons to think twice about going to university

The benefits of going to university are not guaranteed and, of course, there may be other ways to achieve the same benefits. You should, therefore, think twice about going to university, not least because the financial cost of going to university is significant.

- According to the House of Commons Library, students who begin their university course in 2023 and take out a student loan will have average debt of £43,400 when they leave (by the way, according to *The Economist*, tuition fees for university in England are the highest, on average, in the developed world).

- There were recent changes to student loans which means that for students starting their course after 1 August 2023 the threshold at which you start paying your loan is now £25,000 (previously £27,295) and the period in which you are liable to pay off your loan has been extended from 30 years to 40 years (i.e. the loan won't be cancelled until you are, for example, 61 years old, rather than 51). As Martin Lewis, the man behind award-winning website moneysavingexpert.com, said on *Good Morning Britain*, 'For all intents and purposes the vast majority of graduates will be repaying their loans for their entire working lives.'

- If nearly half of graduates will not reach the new threshold of earnings of £25,000 for the first 40 years of their working lives, then there is a question about whether a degree is financially worth it (it may be worth it for other reasons of course).

- A study by Aviva (the insurance company) in 2017 found that parents give on average around £300 per month to their children at university to support them (i.e. a total of around £10,000 over three years).

*A quick note: Tuition fees for university in Scotland and Northern Ireland are lower for residents of those countries than they are for students resident in England and Wales.*

## Reasons for going to uni

The following table looks at each of the benefits of going to university outlined in Chapter 4.1 and provides some context and questions you can ask to 'sense check' whether university would be right for you.

| If your reason to go to uni is... | ... then make sure you do the following: |
|---|---|
| 1. to study a subject you love | Check that the learning experience will be a good one. There is considerable variation between student satisfaction, ranging from 93% down to 76%. Look at The Office for Students website, officeforstudents.org.uk to see the satisfaction rates by course at different universities. Speak to people who did the course (find them on LinkedIn) and ask them directly what they thought of it. |
| 2. to help secure a good career (generally) | Sense check that you need a degree for what you want to do. Overall, graduates earn around 11% more than those who have not got a degree. However, this 'premium' is concentrated on a small number of degrees from a small number of universities (e.g. Finance at the London School of Economics, Maths at Cambridge, Engineering at Imperial College London or Law at Oxford), and there is not (yet) comparison data with those who have completed different kinds of apprenticeships. You should not assume that the average career earnings benefit of getting a degree is greater than that of someone doing a good apprenticeship. A November 2022 study by the Chartered Institute for Personnel Development (CIPD) found that over a third of graduates in the UK (36%) were in lower skilled jobs, i.e. ones where they did not need their degree. A 2018 study by the Office for National Statistics found that 12% of non-graduates were working in graduate jobs: i.e. it is not always essential to have a degree to do a so-called 'graduate job'. Speak to a careers advisor who can help you evaluate whether the traditional university route is appropriate for you. |

| If your reason to go to uni is... | ... then make sure you do the following: |
|---|---|
| 2a. to help secure a good career by acquiring valuable knowledge and skills | Make sure that the knowledge and skills you hope to get are in fact covered by the course. Bear in mind that employers increasingly care less than they used to about academic achievement at university. For example, as reported in *The Times* in December 2022, PwC (along with many other firms) has removed the requirement for graduate entrants to attain a 2:1, saying instead that 'More students will be able to access PwC's programmes as the firm assesses potential instead of academic attainment.' Other employers are also shifting to assessment criteria that are less to do with university achievement and more to do with practical skills that can be of value to the employer. Careers advisors will be a good source of advice. Speak directly to companies as well, attend their online careers days and do your research. |
| 2b. to help secure a good career because it has a 'sandwich year' or industry placement | First, research what industry placements students who are doing the course actually do. Second, ask how many people who do the industry placement go on to full-time related employment. Third, consider whether it is the industry placement (one year) that is the main reason for doing the degree (four years) – if it is, then you may be able to get the advantages of that one year through a 15–18-month long apprenticeship without having to do the other three years (or incur the associated costs) of the degree. |
| 2c. to help secure a good career because you get to do extra-curricular activities that develop work-relevant skills | While many universities have a rich fabric of sports clubs, societies and other entertainments, this is not guaranteed – and, of course, you can still have hobbies without going to university. |

| If your reason to go to uni is... | ... then make sure you do the following: |
| --- | --- |
| 3. to have fun | Think about three things:<br>Once you have factored in tuition fees and living costs, going to uni is quite an expensive way to have fun.<br>Having fun at uni is not guaranteed (any more than it is in any other walk of life); a study by Cibyl with Accenture, Clyde & Co, Imperial College London and Universities UK (called 'Student Mental Health Study 2022') found that 81% of students had experienced some form of mental health difficulty, with 27% saying they were lonely.<br>University does not have a monopoly on this kind of fun: it is completely possible in other options. Indeed, apprentices often have a great social life because they have money to spend. |
| 4. to learn and grow as a person | This does not happen magically – you have to make it happen.<br>Most people, regardless of what they do, will learn and grow as a person between the ages of 18 and 21 – it is a key period in most people's life, when they finish adolescence and become a fully-fledged adult. Perhaps you do not need university to do this and other options will have the same impact. |
| 5. to have the time and space to figure out what you want to do next | It may well be that you can get many of these benefits without going to university. For example, if you took on a series of jobs (whether apprenticeships or not) over a three-year period it is likely you would learn a lot – perhaps even more – about yourself, your preferences and your strengths and weaknesses. |

## 💡 Interesting idea: The apprentice mindset

In my research, I have asked employers how they compare apprentices and graduates. Often they make no distinction between them, seeing them as different but complementary groups of early career employees; certainly none feel that graduates are 'superior' to apprentices.

A number of employers, however, have noted that apprentices often have a mindset that is better suited to the world of work than some graduates.

They note the following attributes in apprentices.

- Apprentices are up for learning – they know they are starting at the beginning; by contrast, some university graduates think that because they have been studying for three years that they have already learned enough.
- Apprentices are ready to 'get their hands dirty', and will undertake tasks, whatever they are, willingly and enthusiastically; graduates, some employers note, can have unrealistic expectations about the kind of things they will be working on, assuming they will be 'above' certain tasks, when in fact these tasks are what the employer needs them to do.
- Apprentices know that the world of work is not like school; by contrast, for some graduates the 'school mindset' (of having learning delivered to you) becomes more entrenched at university. As a result, these graduates struggle even more to adjust to the world of work than if they had gone straight into work from school.
- Apprentices are resilient, and seem to instinctively understand that work, a job and a career will inevitably have ups and downs; graduates, by contrast, sometimes seem to assume that their career will be an inexorable and smooth rise.

While universities are now measured on graduate outcomes and many have good careers and employability support services, they also want to keep current students enrolled and so have an incentive for saying positive things about employment prospects following successful graduation to their students. It is understandable that some of these students may believe that the world beyond university will be easier for them than is the case.

# 4.3 Understanding pro-university bias

Given the mixed picture about university, why is it that it gets such strong support from society? Why do so many teachers, parents and friends and family give such strong support to the idea of you going to university? Why is it that they do not seem to be aware of the downsides, only the upsides?

If you understand what is behind this bias, you will be able to interpret the advice you are getting better, have more productive conversations with people advising you and be more confident about reaching your own conclusions.

There are three reasons why parents (and others of a similar age, such as other relatives and family friends) and your teachers are often so pro-university.

1. Their views of the value of university are based on what was true historically when they were younger.
2. Because of their own experience in relation to university.
3. Because if you attend university they will feel they have succeeded as a parent or teacher.

And there are also three more reasons why teachers in particular are often pro-university.

4. Their university degree is how and why they are in their job.
5. They know how to support you to go to university.
6. They get measured on people going to university.

And there is a final reason why your parents and family may like the idea of you going to university.

7. They don't want you to grow up just yet!

Let's look at each of these in turn.

## 1. An outdated view of the value of university

This is particularly likely to afflict your parents and those advising you who are Gen Xers, (like me) now in their 40s, 50s and 60s.

At the end of the 20th century, it was true that having a degree made a real difference to your employment prospects. That's because the economy was different then, with far fewer options for moving roles, companies and careers – careers moved more slowly, and jobs were typically split between 'graduate roles' and every other role. At the same time, only about 20% of people went to university.

Then, in the 1990s, triggered by the explosion of IT and then boosted by the advent of the internet at the start of the 21st century, there was a huge growth in management-style jobs that employers automatically thought were 'graduate' jobs. It meant that there were more 'graduate' jobs than there were graduates – if you had a degree from a university, it felt like you could pick and choose not just your career, but your employer.

And it was free… (indeed, there were no tuition fees and you could get government grants for your living costs).

No wonder they thought university was a good option back then! But they make the mistake of thinking that things are the same now when, in fact, everything has changed. The economy has changed out of all recognition, mainly driven again by technology (see Chapter 1.1 for a reminder of this). And university is not free any more and now nearly half of all people go. A degree is definitely not the free golden ticket to a guaranteed first job and career that it once was.

## 2. Their own relationship to university

If the person advising you went to university, then they may well have a rose-tinted view about their experience: the memories of being independent and away from parents for the first time, having loads of fun, doing lots of activities, while having lots of free time and few obligations.

They will remember their time at uni as a period when they grew up and became an adult. Perhaps some of their closest friends now are people they met at university. They may even have fond memories of what they studied! In short, they may not be able to imagine their life without having gone to university – and they want you to experience this too.

And if they did not go to university, they may really regret that they did not, either because they feel they never really had the opportunity to go or because they did not pursue it hard enough.

They may well want you to not 'make the same mistake', to miss out on the opportunity that they feel they missed out on.

## 3. Feeling they have succeeded as a teacher or parent

Let's start with teachers.

Schools are often judged on how many of their students end up at university. This is partly because it is easy for the system to measure this and partly because society still has a pro-university bias.

On a personal level, your teachers are likely to want some sort of proof that they have done a good job for you, and you going to university is perhaps the best proof they have.

For parents, too, you getting into university is the almost universally socially accepted way for them to show the world that they have done a 'good job' as your parent. If you go to university, then it implies strongly that you have been educated well (a key 'job' for any parent), that you are confident to leave the home (ditto) and that you are going to have fun (another tick). Plus, they would like that graduation photo to put on the mantelpiece.

Many parents will not feel the same about you getting an apprenticeship. They may even think that other people will 'look down their noses' at your choice. This is changing, however, and a growing number of parents are 'cottoning on' to the fact that a good apprenticeship is every bit as a good university.

There are three further reasons why teachers specifically are likely to have a pro-university bias:

## 4. Their degree is how & why teachers are in their job

The vast majority of teachers will have nearly always have done a degree in the subject they teach, or one very close to it. Indeed, it is because they got a degree in that subject that they have their teaching job. On top of that, because they like the subject so much they want to teach it as a job, it's pretty likely that they really enjoyed their time at university.

So in their minds, getting a degree is both a great thing and directly and inextricably linked to how you get a job. The fact that they then hang out in the staff room with other teachers who have exactly the same opinion reinforces their thinking. It is likely that if you asked them directly they would, of course, say that they know that lots of people get degrees that do not lead directly to their jobs – but the weight and depth of their own personal experience means they carry a deep bias towards going to university.

## 5. Teachers know how to get you to university

People prefer to do things they know they are good at it. Teachers are good at advising students on going to university, whereas they (often) do not know how to advise on apprenticeships.

When it comes to university, they have been through it and the application process themselves, and UCAS provides a familiar process to help students through.

With apprenticeships, on the other hand, many teachers are nervous about the current 'world of work' and have little knowledge or understanding of what an apprenticeship is, let alone how to get one.

So, understandably, they prefer to stick to what they know and, without even realising it, are pointing you towards university for no better reason than it is the option they know best – regardless of whether it is the right one for you.

Now that UCAS includes apprenticeships, I expect that teachers will, over time, become increasingly familiar and comfortable with apprenticeships.

## 6. Teachers get judged on people going to university

Schools are judged on the percentage of pupils going on to university – the measurement system still assumes that uni is the best option (although now this does include degree apprenticeships). Schools often talk about how many of their students go on to university in their brochures and on their websites, whether they are a private school or an inner-city comprehensive.

This means that it is also in the day-to-day conversations teachers have: which of their students is going for university (and in which subjects), and it is a source of pride when their students successfully get to uni. This day-to-day culture and conversation reinforces their pro-university bias.

This is changing too, but slowly, as teachers see their students going into apprenticeships, flourishing in them and then coming back to the school or college to give talks on their experiences.

Finally, there is one more reason why your parents in particular may prefer you to go to university (and it is the one they might be least willing to admit!)…

## 7. Your parents don't want you to grow up just yet!

Some parents will have loved the process of bringing you up and will be anxious about the thought of you being a grown-up, who no longer needs them in quite the same way as they once did. Their instinct to protect and nurture you may remain as strong as when you were a little child.

This can make them anxious about you joining the world of work. They may prefer for you to put that off for another three or four years by going to university, where, although you are no longer their 'baby' you're not yet a fully fledged adult either.

# 4.4 How to handle pro-university bias

If you feel that the people advising you have this pro-university bias, then it is important that you handle it with care. After all, they are trying to help you, and it is best to be able to make your points without it being confrontational and stressful. This is difficult, not least because parents and teachers with this bias reinforce each other: parents listen to teachers who are positive about university, teachers hear positive reinforcement about the value of university back from parents and so the bias is confirmed.

If you feel you are getting this sort of pressure to go to university, gently challenge the people giving you this advice with some of the information in this guidebook.

Here are a few things you can ask them to stimulate a productive conversation.

- Are they aware of how quickly the economy is changing?
- Are they aware of just how many prestigious employers are now hiring people directly as apprentices?
- Are they aware of the sub-optimal outcomes for many graduates from many universities?
- Are they aware of the full financial implications of going to university? (Not just the tuition fees, but also the living costs, debt and missing three years of salary?)
- Are they aware of the benefits of other options, such as apprenticeships? This includes, but should not be limited to, the financial implications.
- Have they read this book? Have they looked at other websites and publications to read the case studies of both employers and apprentices about their experiences?
- If they went to university before 1999, would they have paid £43,000 for those three years? Would they be happy paying (in effect) higher income tax than people who didn't go to university, even if they earned the same amount, because of a student loan?

# 4.5 Other options

Believe it or not, going to uni and doing an apprenticeship are not your only options! There are other options that could be better for you or could be good 'back up' options.

1. Other training that is not an apprenticeship.
2. A regular (i.e. non-apprenticeship) job.
3. Volunteering.
4. Taking time out/a gap year.

Let's look at these in turn:

## 1. Non-apprenticeship training

There are numerous training options outside of apprenticeships.

There are courses you can take at FE (Further Education) colleges, some of which attract government funding, some of which you need to pay for yourself.

The Government is winding down the 'traineeship' programme (which you may still hear about) and has replaced them with 'bootcamps' that serve a similar purpose as traineeships, but with less emphasis on the work experience (the bit that is hardest to arrange). Bootcamps, typically around three months long, are designed to give people an opportunity to get some rapid training and the chance to get to know employers through a combination of employer events and/or shadowing and mentoring. These are available through many of the same training providers who deliver apprenticeships and cover many of the same occupations as apprenticeships (although they major on sectors that have particularly acute skills shortages, such as construction and digital).

They are a good option if you want to try out different occupations or if you are finding it hard to get an apprenticeship and need an extra boost; for example, you can get to know a training provider through the bootcamp who can then put you forward for apprenticeships they are running.

However, while bootcamps are free (you don't have to pay for the training) you do not earn money while you are on them – so you have to be supported or have an alternative source of income.

There are also private training providers offering career starter courses. Some of these are free while others charge fees, which are sometimes quite high (e.g. for coding courses). These can be effective ways to get a step up into the first job of your career. Ask the same demanding questions of these programmes as you would of university or an apprenticeship: How do they work? What is involved? How do they link you to employers? What is their success rate? And can you speak to people who have been through the programme?

## 2. Going into a regular (non-apprenticeship) job

This is a completely acceptable way to start your working life. Some jobs do not need prior experience, and many will allow you to get started and learn as you go, without the support of a formal apprenticeship.

The upside of this route: it is simple and does not require any further study. It is also possible for non-apprenticeship jobs to become apprenticeships once your employer has got to know you and if you show an inclination for going down this route.

There are downsides, however: there is a risk that a job like this may not have the structure or progression to move your career forward; you may not gain any qualifications; you may find yourself 'bouncing' from one such job to another; and there is no mechanism in place to help you progress and increase your earnings.

In other words, it may be a job, but it may not lead to a career.

Often people will take on a regular 'non-career' job while they are applying for apprenticeships in order to reduce the financial pressure.

## 3. Volunteering & unpaid work experience

This is a viable short-term option if you are not under immediate pressure to earn money.

Volunteering can bring you the following benefits.

- It can give you valuable work experience to include on job/apprenticeship applications and to talk about at interviews.
- People you meet while volunteering may introduce you to opportunities that you would not have found out about otherwise, or might have contacts who can.
- It will keep you active while you are waiting for other opportunities.
- It can be satisfying and fun.

Ideally this would be in a field that is related to the career you are interested in, but even if it isn't, the experience still has a lot of value.

However, not least because it is not paid, be sure to have a clear plan for how you will combine volunteering with either other paid work and/or your apprenticeship and job hunting activities. Perhaps put a time limit on it, to ensure you do not drift along.

## 4. Taking some time out/a gap year

You may feel that after spending what feels like your whole life at school you are not yet ready to throw yourself into something else. Or maybe you have always wanted to travel the world.

Taking some time out is a good option: when you are in your late teens and early 20s you are unlikely to have significant responsibilities to other people; you have energy; and you are more likely to have a sense of adventure than later in your life. You can use this time period to go and do incredible things and create amazing memories. It will give you the opportunity to create your own independent self and potentially forge relationships for life.

However, there are risks associated with this. A short break to have some time out can drift into being a big break, to being a never-ending 'break' that can be hard to end.

So, if you are going to take this option, make sure you:

- have a plan – don't just drift
- earn some money – even if it is a casual job, having some money is seriously useful (perhaps to save a bit so you can do some exciting travelling). And, of course, being in a job, even a casual one, is still valid work experience and will keep you learning
- give yourself a time limit – and stick to it. Maybe ask members of your family and friends to keep you on track with this.

# Section 4 summary:
# What you need to know about university and other options

Going to uni is often presented as the 'default' post-school option. Numbers of people going to university remain high at over 500,000 people a year. Many graduates have good employment outcomes and a good experience. However, the picture is highly varied, with some having a poor experience and little positive impact on their earnings. Debt on leaving uni remains high on average at just over £43,000.

There are good reasons to go to university:

- to study a subject you love
- to secure a good career
- to have fun
- to learn and grow as a person
- to have the time and space to figure out what you want to do next.

For each of these proposed benefits it is important to make sure that the universities and courses you are applying for will deliver what you want them to, and to think about whether there are other ways in which you can achieve these same benefits – university does not have a monopoly on them, and certainly does not guarantee them.

It is important to understand, given this mixed picture, why there is such a strong pro-university bias among many of the people advising you. There are a number of reasons behind this:

- Their views of the value of university are based on what was true historically when they were younger
- Because they have such a positive memory of their university experience; or, if they did not go, they are regretful and do not want you to miss out like they did
- Because it makes them feel they have succeeded as a parent or teacher.

And for teachers in particular:

- Their degree is how and why they are in their job
- They know how to support you to get into university
- They get judged on people getting in to university.

And for family members, especially protective parents (!):

- They don't want you to grow up just yet! And going to university rather than going out into the adult world of work gives them another few years of looking after you, albeit more remotely.

You can navigate these pro-university biases in a sensitive and productive way, by engaging with adults who have it with positive questions and equipped with the information from sources such as this guidebook.

University and apprenticeships are not your only options. Others are:

- other training that is not an apprenticeship
- a regular (i.e. non-apprenticeship) job
- volunteering
- taking time out/a gap year.

They each have pros and cons and are worth considering as long as you have a clear plan for each one.

## APPRENTICE CASE STUDY: LILI WILSON

Until recently, in order to get into the publishing industry you needed a combination of the 'right' degree and, usually, some personal contacts who already worked in the industry. But publishing is yet another sector going through huge changes, as publishing companies realise that their traditional ways of hiring talent are not good enough: they need to attract and recruit different people in order to stay competitive and to be as diverse as the general public who buy their books.

Lili Wilson is a great example of this. Lili joined Faber & Faber as a business administration apprentice two years ago. She started, though, down a very traditional route: under pressure from her school she went to university: 'They certainly made it seem as though uni is the only option.'

She completed two years at university before deciding that it was not offering her enough, especially when her studies all went online because of the Covid-19 pandemic. Lili instead took the plunge, dropped out (knowing that she could always return to uni at some point later in life) and started searching for alternatives. 'I was looking at everything: apprenticeships, internships, traineeships. My English teacher had told me that I would not get into publishing because it was too competitive. However, I did my research and found apprenticeships in publishing – and I started applying. I wasn't successful with my application for an apprenticeship at Penguin, but I didn't give up.'

She looked at an alternative route, and secured a traineeship with training provider LDN, and with their support, was able to step up into an apprenticeship with Faber & Faber. Since she has started her career there she has had broad exposure to many different aspects of publishing, from editorial, to operational to their corporate initiative to make themselves as environmentally friendly as possible and, now, in sales.

She says that the apprenticeship qualification and support has been hugely valuable. 'I have learned lots about project management and personal money management – not something I learned at uni. I have also learned a huge amount about the fundamentals of business.' And it's not just the 'formal' side of things that have made a difference: her network of fellow apprentices have been an ongoing source of support and help: 'It's so cool to have a professional network with people who I wouldn't have met otherwise.'

Her advice for people considering their options? 'There are so many more options than uni – make sure you look at them all. Apprenticeships are great if you can't afford university and want to get into an industry that is hard to get into.' She now often hears from her friends who completed their degrees how much they wish they had looked at the apprenticeship option as well.

## EMPLOYER CASE STUDY: THE NHS

If you want a sign of the rise of apprenticeships in the last decade, look no further than the NHS: in 2016, 1,186 people started an apprenticeship in the NHS; in 2022 that number was 25,000.

Apprenticeships within the NHS can be found across the country, from Level 2 all the way up to Level 7, across the 350 (!) different occupations this massive and complex organisation employs. These include medical occupations, such as nursing and clinical staff, but also roles in HR, finance, administration, facilities management and digital, data and technology (where there is about to be an even greater push for more apprenticeships).

As Lucy Hunte, the National Programme Manager for NHS Apprenticeships says, 'Apprenticeships in the NHS are now "business as usual".' NHS Trusts up and down the country are finding consistent benefits from using apprenticeships to attract new talent and develop existing staff. 'Apprenticeships are great for retention: 97% of people who start a nursing apprenticeship complete it successfully – way higher than through our traditional training and hiring routes.'

That's not the only reason: 'Apprenticeships are amazing for widening participation, opening up NHS roles to as many people as possible, whatever their background. It enables people who might not otherwise be able to afford to be unpaid while getting trained to become skilled and to progress – which also means we open roles up to local people. It's win-win.' She points to the growth of new organisations to help people thrive in apprenticeships, such as the Association of Apprentices and the Multicultural Apprenticeship Alliance, and of initiatives within the NHS to help people get to apprenticeship roles in rural and coastal areas where there is poor local transport.

Lucy is keen to emphasise to young people currently at school that there are really great options for them as apprentices in the NHS – even if teachers are 'programmed' to direct students towards university, especially if they are academically successful. 'There are still lots of myths to bust about apprenticeships. That's one of the reasons we are so excited about the launch of the Medical Doctor apprenticeship – you can now become a fully qualified doctor via an apprenticeship, and it is the exact same degree just funded differently.'

She also points out that it is not like applying for university: 'You need to tailor your applications – employers will know if you are just firing off the same application to lots of employers. You need to research the specific organisations you are applying to and adjust your application: every NHS Trust has their own values and priorities, if you can reflect these in how you apply, you will really boost your chances.'

She has some other really valuable advice for anyone considering an apprenticeship: 'You need to be realistic about the challenges of juggling a full-time job and getting a qualification at the same time. It is tough, and a real commitment. On the plus side, you will become an expert in time management, a vital skill for any career in the 21st century.'

The future will see even more apprenticeships in the NHS across even more occupations. Lucy's team is about to launch a big push to increase the number of DDAT apprenticeships (Digital, Data and Technology), and in 2024 the first apprentices will begin their Medical Doctor apprenticeship programmes, on the road to fully qualifying as a doctor. 'We could have four times as many apprentices as we do today. It's a really exciting future.'

# Section 5
# Deciding whether to do
# an apprenticeship

# Introduction to Section 5: Deciding whether to do an apprenticeship

We have explored a bit more what the main options are, focusing especially on apprenticeships and going to university: their pros and cons, the key things to think about and how to interpret what other people are telling you (especially if you think they have a pro-university bias).

Now we turn to focus on you, and how you can make the right decision for **you**.

Use the Apprenticeship Decision Tool available at indigo.careers to help you weigh up your options, including an assessment of the financial implications.

This section starts by reminding you that no decision is for life, and that whatever you decide to do next does not prevent you changing your mind and doing something else in the future.

The section then looks at the following questions in turn.

- Is it a good time for you to embark on an apprenticeship?
- Do you have what it takes to succeed in an apprenticeship?
- What kind of apprenticeships should you consider?
  - What is important to you?
  - What do you enjoy doing?
  - What are your strengths and weaknesses?

If after all this you still want to do an apprenticeship, read Sections 6 and 7 which look at the process of finding and applying for apprenticeships.

# 5.1 Why this decision is not forever

Whatever and however you decide, it is really important that you understand this: your decision now (or at any time) is not a decision forever; whatever you decide to do now does not determine the rest of your life.

So don't worry about having to get this decision right. There is no 'perfect' decision, and there is no way of knowing for sure what a better decision would have been.

This may run somewhat contrary to what you have been told up until now. Each time you come up to a set of exams or tests, it is likely that your teachers – and maybe your parents too – have said that you *must* do well in them.

Whether it's GCSEs, A levels or BTECs, the message is the same: succeed in these exams and (somehow) you will get through a magical gateway into a wonderful future where all will be well, where amazing opportunities will flow your way and where success in life will be assured: you never need to worry again.

And conversely (they let you believe), if you do not succeed at these exams, you will miss out forever and instead experience a life of hardship and difficulty.

No wonder stress at school is so prevalent!

Of course, once you've got through GCSEs, the message changes to focus on passing your A levels; and once you've got through them, it's all about getting to university; and at university it's all about getting a great result in your exams and getting a great job… and so on and so on.

I'm here to tell you: none of this is true.

There is no 'magical gateway' now, or at any point in time, at any point in your career. This includes any apprenticeship you might do, any job you get, any promotion you earn and any pay rise you are awarded.

And that's okay. You can flunk some exams. You can drop out of uni. You can drop out of an apprenticeship. You can try different things in life. You are likely to switch careers several times in your working life, so do not think for a moment that whatever you choose to do now – whether it's going to university, doing an apprenticeship or anything else – is a permanent decision.

Here are five things to remember as you approach your choice about what to do next.

i. No choice is forever. If you start doing something, you can always switch. Plenty of the case studies of apprentices in this book have done just that.

ii. You only really learn by doing (life is one long apprenticeship!). You will never know whether a choice you might make is a good one or not if it stays as a theoretical choice – you have to try it out for real. Do not be afraid, therefore, to try things out as a way to test and learn.

iii. Don't aim for a 'perfect' choice – if you keep trying to find the perfect choice, you will consume enormous amounts of time and energy without any guarantee of success, and you run the very real risk that in your quest for the 'perfect' opportunity you miss out on lots of good or very good opportunities. You may find that the 'perfect' opportunity turns out to be less than perfect. Instead, aim for a good opportunity. You will soon learn, once you have got into it, whether it is good, very good or not good.

iv. Learn, learn, learn – even from the choices that turn out to be a bit rubbish (maybe especially learn from these ones!). What about it was bad? What did you miss when you were making the choice? What do you wish you had asked about? What else would you do differently? Answer these questions and you will come away with invaluable knowledge and wisdom for the next choice you have to make.

v. Try to enjoy the ride – life is unpredictable, and despite your best efforts there will be downs as well as ups. Make sure you enjoy the ups, don't worry too much about the downs – they will pass. The more you can embrace the fact that life is like this, the more you will find yourself able to roll with things, and the more enjoyable you will find the whole experience.

# 5.2 Is now a good time for you to embark on an apprenticeship?

Even if you know that the choice you are about to make is not for life you do, nonetheless, still need to make a choice: do you want to go to university, try to get an apprenticeship or go for one of the other options mentioned in Chapter 4.5?

Here are three key questions to help you 'frame' your decision on whether now is the right time for you to do an apprenticeship.

1. How do you feel about money? Do you want (or need) to earn money now? How do you feel about debt?
2. How ready do you feel you are for the 'real'/adult world?
3. How clear are you about what you want to do?

Let's look at each of these in a bit more detail.

## 1. Do you want or need to earn money now?

Like many, you may be motivated by the prospect of earning money and building a career as soon as possible. You might want to get a 'head start' relative to your peers.

Or you may not have a choice: not working (or earning) while doing a degree is simply not an option.

If either or both of the above applies to you, then going straight for a job or an apprenticeship will be a good option for you.

How you feel about debt is also important here. If you are comfortable with debt and paying it back over a long period of time then you may be happy to take out a Student Loan. If you are very lucky, then you may not even have to worry about taking on any debt to go to university.

But if you do not have enough financial resources to cover university costs and you are uncomfortable with debt, then it will not make sense to go to university.

Take some time to think about how you really feel about money. Talk to others to help you work out what you think.

**Download the Financial analysis Tool available at indigo. careers/undestanding_apprenticeships** to work out what the financial implications are for you from going to university and from doing an apprenticeship.

## 2. Are you ready to operate in the 'real'/ adult world?

Some people just want to get on with it. They don't want to delay getting started in their adult life. They may already feel comfortable and familiar with the adult world of work. Others are less confident and even a bit daunted by the thought of going into a job when you are still young, yet motivated to give it a go and prove themselves.

Many of the case study apprentices in this book have said how valuable this part of their experience has been: confronting the reality of the 'world of work' at a young age, and overcoming the challenges involved sooner rather than later. They believe the confidence boost they experience means they progress quicker and further in their career than if they had delayed and gone to university.

But some people do not feel ready for work yet. They feel that they do not yet know enough about who they are or what they want to do to take that step. They may feel they are ready to leave home, but not yet ready to take on 'full on' adult responsibilities and roles. Continuing in full-time education may be the right choice for them.

The key here is to take your time to figure out what is right for you: either to get going now in the world of work, or to delay a few years.

## 3. How clear are you about the career you want?

Some people know what they want to do in their career from a very early age, others might know by the time they leave school and others take much longer to work it out (if they ever do!).

If you are already clear on what you want to do, that is great. Your decision is then simply about the best route into that career: apprenticeship, university degree or perhaps another option.

But if, like many people, you are not yet clear about what you want to do, rest reassured that this is completely normal! There are so many possibilities and options, and with your head focused on exams, you can be forgiven for not having a clear and settled view of 'what next'.

Remember that whatever you decide to do now does not close off other options later: if you go for an apprenticeship now, you can always move on to either a degree apprenticeship or a normal degree later, and vice versa. Your other options – a non-apprenticeship job, non-apprenticeship training and taking time out – are available throughout your life.

Weigh up the pros and cons of the various options carefully. Here are some pointers if you are unsure about your career in relation to your main options:

- *Going to university when you are unsure about your career*
  - ✔ Benefits
    - ◆ It will buy you time to think and reflect on what you might want to do.
    - ◆ Universities do not mind much if you are unsure – as long as you are interested and motivated enough to stay for the duration of the course.
    - ◆ You get to see how people in the years ahead of you interact with the jobs market and you can learn from their experience.
    - ◆ You can get specialist careers advice provided by the university.
    - ◆ And, perhaps most valuably, you can undertake low pressure part-time jobs, holiday internships and potentially industry placements to help you test and learn what you might want to do when you leave.

✗ Downsides

◆ Three years is quite a long time.

◆ It is expensive: you are only earning what you get from part-time jobs/internships/placement year and you are having to pay tuition fees (whether upfront or through debt).

◆ If, after university, you decide that you want to do an apprenticeship, you may find yourself unable to get one if there is too much overlap between the content of your degree and the content of the apprenticeship.

◆ You may be as unclear at the end of your degree course as you were at the beginning.

◆ You may feel stuck and obliged to 'stick it out'.

● *Doing an apprenticeship when you are unsure about your career*

✔ Benefits

◆ Many apprenticeships are only 12–18 months long: the commitment required is shorter than going to university.

◆ You will quickly learn about yourself, your preferences and your strengths and weaknesses in a real work environment: these learnings will help you assess your suitability not just for the occupation your apprenticeship is in, but for your career aspirations more generally.

◆ You will earn a wage and not incur any fees.

◆ You will get work experience that you can transfer to whatever your next job is.

✗ Downsides

◆ If you are unsure when you apply (and it shows) employers may be less willing to offer you an apprenticeship.

◆ You may end up stuck in a job that you know is not right for you and feel obliged to complete the apprenticeship.

- *Doing more further education (not university or an apprenticeship) when you are unsure*
  - ✔ Benefits
    - ◆ Courses are typically shorter, which means you can try things out.
    - ◆ They are sometimes free or inexpensive.
    - ◆ You are usually able to maintain part-time work, potentially in the same field as your field of study.
    - ◆ It is a 'low pressure' way (as you are not committed for long or financially) to buy time for thinking and planning.
  - ✗ Downsides
    - ◆ Not earning (unless also doing part-time jobs).
    - ◆ Qualifications may not be valued by employers.
    - ◆ Feels like a less certain route to a career.
- *Taking time out/going straight into a job when you are unsure about your career*
  - ✔ Benefits
    - ◆ Getting a regular job or series of part-time jobs gives you a 'low pressure' way to learn about yourself in a work environment.
    - ◆ You will earn a wage and not incur debt.
    - ◆ You will get work experience.
    - ◆ There are lots of opportunities to have fun as a young person earning money and without many responsibilities (albeit without the support structure of a university or employer investing in you for the longer term).
  - ✗ Downsides
    - ◆ You may not gain any insight into what career you would like to pursue.
    - ◆ You won't have achieved a further/higher qualification.
    - ◆ You may not have enhanced your 'pitch' for when you want to start a career.

If you are unclear about what you want to do with your career, don't worry; take your time to consider what a good option will be for you, safe in the knowledge that you will learn more over time about your long-term preferences.

# 5.3 What attributes do you need to succeed in an apprenticeship?

There are five key attributes that seem to be the predictors of success for a young person doing an apprenticeship, regardless of the occupation.

1. Being interested *enough* in the occupation and sector that the apprenticeship is in.
2. Valuing learning.
3. Being willing and able to take instructions.
4. Being organised (or at least prepared to get organised).
5. Being resilient (enough).

## 1. Being interested *enough* in the occupation & sector

It is important that you care about the work you do (this is true not just for your apprenticeship but for your whole working life). You do not need to be 100% passionate about it, or care about it more than other things in your life – what is important is that you are interested *enough*.

This is because if you care *enough* about the work your apprenticeship involves, you will find it easier to motivate yourself, easier to learn (because your brain is naturally switched on) and easier to overcome the inevitable challenges, large and small, that come with the territory of work.

Here are the signs that you are probably 'interested enough' in an occupation or sector.

- You have done and enjoyed relevant work experience.
- You have talked to employers about it and found the conversations interesting.
- You have been thinking about it for some time.
- You have talked to friends and family about it.
- You have spotted a connection between it and something you enjoy doing.

## 2. Valuing learning

All apprenticeships are about learning.

To succeed in an apprenticeship, you have to be open to learning, whether that is formal or informal, structured or unstructured, taught by someone else or self-taught, online or in person. If you are, then every day you will see things that will enable you to improve and progress. You will find that completing the tasks associated with the qualification is easy and natural. You will embrace and enjoy your apprenticeship.

But if you are not open to learning, you will find an apprenticeship hard work, and it is unlikely to be a good option for you.

## 3. Being willing & able to take instructions

Remember, an apprenticeship is not just a mechanism for learning – it is a job. That means you will have a line manager (who will have their own line manager, and so on, all the way up to the chief executive of the organisation). The role of your line manager is to get the people reporting to them (including you) to successfully achieve things in line with what their line manager and the organisation as a whole want. So line managers have to tell the people reporting to them what they want them to do – and they then need to make sure these people do it.

That means that to be successful in your apprenticeship, you need to be willing and able to take instructions from others.

Being 'willing' means you do not mind when someone tells you what to do. It means not taking it personally if those instructions are sometimes delivered in a brusque way. It means not resenting being told what to do.

If you are someone who, perhaps through a series of poor experiences, does not like taking instructions from other people, then you might struggle with an apprenticeship (in fact, you might struggle with being employed full stop!).

Being able to take instructions means that you understand what other people are saying and can interpret what they really want. Not all people give instructions with complete clarity! You need to be prepared to ask questions that will help you to understand your instructions and give others confidence.

## 4. Being organised enough

Being organised is a great attribute for every job, and indeed for other aspects of your life. Some people are naturally more organised than others. Don't worry if you are not very organised: you just need to be organised *enough* to ensure you get through your work and your learning tasks. Lots of apprentices say that they were not organised or good at time management at the start of their apprenticeships, but they learned these skills as their apprenticeship progressed.

Here are the things to focus on.

- Keep your work calendar/diary up to date, and always aim to be at least five minutes early for every meeting.
- Take notes in meetings (always have a notepad, whatever apprenticeship you are in), especially on the actions you need to do (do not rely on your memory – you will be amazed at how difficult it is to hold in your head all the things you need to do).
- If you have forgotten something, ask – much better to ask and be seen to have a less than perfect memory than to not ask, not get the task done and be seen as careless or incompetent.

## 5. Being resilient enough

Doing an apprenticeship is not an easy option. You are in a work environment where what you do matters. You will experience setbacks, whether that is because things do not work out the way you thought or because colleagues or customers are abrasive (the world of work always comes with different pressures!); or it could be in your learning, where some things are just harder to absorb than others.

You do not need to be super-tough, but you do need to be able to roll with some of these kind of experiences and, ideally, use them as an opportunity to learn even more. You need to be resilient.

## Helpful, but not essential, attributes

There are also some other things that you may have heard you need to have and that you may be worried about – but that are less important than you think.

- Social skills: it is helpful if you can get on well with lots of different people at work, but that is not why an employer hires you or invests in your skills. They hire you because of what you can do for them, now and in the future.

- Academically smart: if you are willing to learn and are enthusiastic about what you do, you will not need to be academically smart; if you are willing to learn you will soon figure out how to get things done effectively and efficiently.

- Being an extrovert: while it may feel good in your interview or on the first day at work to be confident enough to introduce yourself to new people and to make conversation, it is not essential (at all); often people like it when new arrivals are not 'in their face'. So being an introvert or shy can even be an advantage.

- Being 'normal': firstly, there is no such thing as 'normal'! Second, lots of organisations are looking for people who will give them a different perspective or insight that they do not already have – in other words, being a bit unusual can be a bonus.

- Maintaining eye contact and a firm handshake: while it is good to maintain some eye contact and to have a reasonable handshake (if that's what is expected), this is not what makes you a good candidate or apprentice.

- Coming across as 'passionate' about the job: if you really are passionate about the apprenticeship, you should say so; but you do not have to be – it is enough at this stage of your career to be interested and enthusiastic.

## 💡 Interesting idea: The growth mindset

'I can't do that.'

'Yet.'

Those three letters – y-e-t – could be the most important in your career.

This is because they signal strongly to your brain that it is still able to learn to do something that it cannot at the moment. And this is a crucial aspect of being human: your brain really can change and, in doing so, enable you to do something new, to do something better and/or to do it quicker.

Y-e-t means the world is full of possibilities: just because you cannot do something now, does not mean you cannot do it in the future.

If you embrace the possibility of being able to do things you cannot do now, you will learn and grow, you will find yourself able to do new things and you will find yourself with (justified) confidence that you can navigate the world successfully.

This is what is meant by a growth mindset – the attitude that you can grow and develop, that you are not limited to what you can do at this particular moment.

The concept was created by the Stanford University academic Carol Dweck who did a series of famous experiments that showed that if you think your talents are 'fixed' – that there is nothing you can do about them – you are less likely to learn, more likely to take things badly when they go wrong and likely to be less confident and resilient.

If you have a growth mindset, you will be unafraid of new things. Keep hold of this mindset for as long as you can!

If you do not have a growth mindset, remind yourself that you do not have a growth mindset – yet – because you can change this too.

Think about something you can do now (such as riding a bike, baking a cake, setting up social media accounts, etc.). Now think back to a time when you couldn't do it. How did you get between the two? By learning, by taking a risk, and perhaps by having someone to help you. What is true for that aspect of your life can be true for almost everything else. You can have a growth mindset if you want one!

# 5.4 What kind of apprenticeship might be right for me?

So...

- if you like the idea of doing an apprenticeship,
- if you are in the right situation to do one in terms of money, readiness for the world of work and in relation to how clear you are about your career and
- if you believe you have what it takes

... you are ready for this chapter, which is all about helping you to figure out which of the many thousands of apprenticeships out there are the ones you should be looking at.

Some of these questions relate to your broader career goals and are not just about apprenticeships. There are many good books on careers and lots of people who are there to advise you, not least careers advisors. Make sure you talk to them!

This chapter is here to help you with those reflections and conversations, in order that you maximise the chances of getting into an apprenticeship and of having a brilliant career.

In particular, you should try to understand four things about yourself.

1. What is important to you and what you want to achieve in life. Do you want to earn lots of money? Do you want a good work-life balance? And so on.
2. What you enjoy doing. Do you like working with people? Do you like to solve problems? Do you like to work with your hands?
3. What are you good at? Often this is very similar to what you enjoy doing, but not always.
4. What are your weaknesses? It is worth knowing what you find difficult or what upsets you.

There is no mechanistic formula that will lead you from these questions directly to the apprenticeship that will be perfect for you – life is not that simple! But if you take time to think about them, then you will find that you will naturally be able to assess your options more effectively and with less stress.

Be as honest with yourself as possible – even if that is not always easy. You do not have to share your thoughts with anyone else if you do not want to. But if you are not honest with yourself on these things, you could find yourself in an apprenticeship and a career that isn't right for you, however brilliant it sounded to everyone else.

By the way, there is a good chance that you won't actually know the answer to all these questions. That's okay (and understandable – you are right at the start of your career!). The key is honesty and being ready to learn about yourself.

## Interesting idea: Career research

You may well have received advice to 'Do your research!'

And indeed, you most definitely should.

But what does this 'research' look like? Are you doing it 'right'? How should you get going with it?

Here is a very short guide to help you if you are wondering how to go about it or get started by looking at how you make a decision, what your sources are and your process.

**1. How you make a 'decision': rational and emotional factors**
Ultimately, only you can make the decision about what you are going to do. That decision in the end will come down to a combination of emotions – things you will feel about an option – and rational factors – things you will think about an option. Humans like to think that they are mainly rational. In fact, there is growing evidence to suggest that ultimately it is our emotions that are the real decision makers for us, albeit influenced by our rational thinking.

As a writer called Antonio Damasio famously said, 'We are not thinking beings that feel, we are feeling beings that think.'

So, do as much rational research as you can, and then trust your instincts, your 'gut', your emotions.

**2. Sources for your research**
Your sources are the different places you can get useful information and insight. These are likely to be the following.

● What you have seen and heard yourself – this is the source you should initially trust least. Why? Because while you will be extremely tempted to feel that you have already got lots of information, it is almost certain that you will start with only a very partial view. There is a psychological term for this: 'availability bias', which is a fancy way of saying that we prefer to believe that the information we already have is all we need – it suits our lazy brains to think they do not need to do more research!

● People you know – friends and family can add lots; although they will have limited information individually, speak to enough of them and you will gather a rich and varied picture. And if they know you well they will be able to give you thoughts and insights into what might be right for you.

● Professional advice – your careers advisor(s) will be professionally trained and many teachers will also be good at providing advice; remember that teachers may have their own biases and preferences, some careers advisors too, even if they have been trained to be objective (in the end, even the most professional person is still human!).

● Websites and publications: there are the 'official' ones, such as the National Careers Service https://nationalcareers.service.gov.uk/ and UCAS (ucas.com), but there are many others as well, such as https://icould.com/, The Prince's Trust and prospects.ac.uk. Search online for 'good careers advice' or, if you are feeling more adventurous, set up a ChatGPT account and ask it to find and describe the best sources of careers advice in the UK.

### 3. Your process

*Step 1*: Start by looking far and wide, don't worry about having very little structure at this point, just go to as many sources as you can. You will naturally find yourself getting a 'feel' for which sources are good and which ones work for you. You will also start to notice things and start asking questions. This is when you can move on to Step 2...

*Step 2*: Start noting down things you find interesting, potential options, ideas and the things you want to know more about. Review them and organise them.

*Step 3*: Go back to the sources that you liked from Step 1, and use them to start answering the questions you now have.

*Step 4*: Write down your initial conclusions, remembering that these will continuously change and evolve as you go through further research and decision making.

If you do these four steps, using a range of sources, you will have a really solid research base to help you make your decision.

## 1. What is important to you in life?

Here are some examples of things that could be important to you. There is no judgement between them – they are all valid – you just need to think about which ones apply to you and which ones do not.

- *Recognition*: You want to do something for which people will thank you or congratulate you, or to be well known for something (maybe even famous!).

- *Helping others*: You want to do your best for your fellow human beings, whether that's a job 'changing the world' or perhaps just 'doing your bit'.

- *Status*: You want to do well compared to your peers and others, and be seen to do well by them and by others.

- *Money*: We all need enough money to live, but this is something different – you want to have the power, the control and the status that comes with financial wealth.

- *Family*: You would like to be in a strong and stable relationship, perhaps have children and be able to spend time with your extended family, providing and receiving support.

- *Low-stress*: You want to avoid uncertainty or high pressure situations and you want to be in control of key aspects of your life.

- *Excitement*: On the other hand, having everything steady and stable to the point of predictable and boring can for many people also be something to avoid; wanting to see the world, having varied and even unpredictable experiences and trying out different things is a common aspiration.

Which of these is most important to you? Or is it something else altogether? Of course, it could be a blend of more than one thing.

Knowing what your aspirations are will help you to judge what sort of roles and employers are likely to be right for you. It will also help you to judge whether to persist in a job when you are going through a tough time or to take the plunge and move on.

But it is not just about finding an apprenticeship in a career that will provide what is important to you. You need to make sure it is in a field that you want to belong in. You have to enjoy what you do, which is the second of the four things you need to know about yourself…

## 2. What do you like doing?

It is really important to be honest about what you like doing. There is no 'moral' judgement here. The key is to make sure you don't end up in an apprenticeship that's not right for you, where you are required to do something that you really do not like doing.

Of course, all jobs – and therefore all apprenticeships – are likely to have some elements that you do not like. This question is about what you think will overall be acceptable to you, given your aspirations (see above).

And as is the case with anything where you have to make a judgement – ultimately a 'gut feel' – the more consideration you give it, and the more structured your thinking around it, the better your judgement will be.

Here are some of the things you should consider when thinking about what you are good at.

- *Socialising*: Do you enjoy meeting people for the first time and having to figure out a way to interact with them? Do you find it interesting to find out about people, and do you enjoy being asked questions as they get to know you?

- *Organising*: Do you like to plan what you and others are going to do, working through systems and processes to get things arranged? Do you like to communicate planning and plans? Do you enjoy keeping track of how things are progressing and stepping in to make sure they happen as planned?

- *Creativity*: Do you like to create new things from scratch or by combining things in new ways? This could be new written things (articles for websites or reports, for example), or perhaps video and audio content, or new designs for products and services that others might benefit from. It could also be events, from business conferences to plays in a theatre. Perhaps you like observing how something is done and coming up with better ways to do it. Often creativity is about joining together in teams to make something new.

- *Working with tools*: Working with tools is one of the things that distinguishes humans from pretty much every other species (some primates and other mammals also use very basic tools – but in nothing like the way we do) – so using tools is a really strong expression of what it means to be human. There are lots of different types of tools.

◆ Tools to change the physical world around us, whether that's in construction, engineering or manufacturing.

◆ Tools to ensure machines and other systems are working as they should, like those in manufacturing plants, our transport infrastructure or our methods of producing and distributing energy to our homes and businesses.

◆ Tools to manage information and data (i.e. computer and internet technology).

- *Problem solving*: Do you relish being presented with a problem to solve? Lots of jobs exist to solve others' problems: anything that involves spotting a problem and diagnosing it, gathering information and analysing it, applying rules and procedures to a new situation, trying out different approaches, and working with others to get their perspectives – all of these are problem-solving activities.

- *Caring*: Many people are motivated by a concern for other living things, whether fellow human beings, animals or indeed plants. The sense of tending and nurturing another complex living being can be hugely motivating.

- *Selling and persuading*: It is a permanent feature of human life that there are products and services that could be really useful to people who do not yet know about them. This knowledge gap can only be bridged by someone who is able to explain and persuade: a salesperson. You may be someone who loves this sort of challenge, and who gets a thrill when you successfully persuade someone of something.

- *Routine or variety*: Some careers, and apprenticeships, have a set pattern every day; others vary significantly from one day, one week or one month to the next; and there are others that are in between. You should think about what you prefer: do you crave 'new' experiences and challenges? Or do you enjoy a routine that enables you to slowly get better and better without throwing up surprises?

- *Working as part of a team or working independently*: Some people love to work with others – they get energy from them, they love the interaction and/or they are nervous about working solo; other people are the exact opposite, and many people are in-between (and it is likely to vary depending on the situation and their mood at the time); be aware of your preferences in this regard.

- *Working with numbers*: Some people just love numbers. This doesn't mean the same as maths as you have learned it at school – but understanding how *quantity* (i.e. numbers) is important and getting satisfaction from working with numbers to deliver business or other organisational outcomes is of real value to many employers.

- *Writing*: Words remain a crucial part of most business settings, whether that is writing words that get other people to do things, or that accurately capture and assess things so that people can take better decisions. If you enjoy working with words, then this is likely to be a valuable skill for many potential organisations.

## 3. What you are good at?

The truth is that for most people, what they enjoy doing for work is typically what they are good at too.

When it comes to hobbies this isn't always true: you might really enjoy something but not be very good at it: not every one who loves dancing is Beyoncé, not everyone who loves painting is a budding Michelangelo, nor is every Sunday golfer as good as Tiger Woods – but you can still love what you do for leisure and relaxation.

But it is much rarer in the world of work to do something that you love but that you are not very good at. This is because if you are not very good at it, you are unlikely to get or keep a job for very long.

There is an exception: *right at the start of your career* it is possible for you to love something but not be very good at it. This is because if you love something enough to be able to learn, quickly and diligently, then you can, quite rapidly, become good at it too – good enough to sustain not just a job but to launch a career.

So it *is* possible for you to go for an apprenticeship where you do not have strengths (yet) as long as you truly love it enough to overcome the extra hurdles in your way.

It is also possible that you have strengths in things that you may not particularly enjoy doing. For example, you may be naturally good at writing or be really good at dealing with customers, even if it these are not things you particularly enjoy doing.

Just because you are good at something does not mean that you should automatically pick a career and apprenticeship in that; it is important that you enjoy it too.

Where you identify your strengths, cherish them and nurture them. Do not be complacent and assume that they will always be strengths. Be proud of them, but be humble. Always think about how you can enhance them and why and how they might be of use to potential employers.

## 4. What are your weaknesses?

You may often hear the advice that you need to know your weaknesses as well as your strengths. It is useful to know them, but don't worry about them too much, certainly not at this stage. It is likely to be a better use of your time and energy to focus on making the most of your strengths than trying to 'fix' your weaknesses.

The most important weaknesses to focus on fixing are those that either dull your enjoyment of something or make your strengths less powerful; for example, not paying enough attention to detail.

However, if you know what your weaknesses are, you will be better able to navigate your way through your apprenticeship (and the rest of your career), because you can avoid situations where your weaknesses would matter, you can minimise their impact if they do come into play and you can communicate to colleagues so they can help you.

It is worth checking whether your emotions are such that they may not suit a particular occupation. For example, if you are uncomfortable or if it upsets you if other people are abrupt or aggressive with you, then think about what that means if, for example, you are going into a job where you will have to deal with members of the public.

## 💡 Interesting idea: 'Ikigai'

Ikigai is a Japanese concept that describes achieving a great balance in your life by doing what is right for you (there is no exact translation into English).

There are four aspects to this.

1. Do something that you love.
2. Do something that the world needs.
3. Do something that you can be paid for.
4. Do what you are good at.

If you have all four of these, then you have ikigai.

The following diagram is how it is often presented:

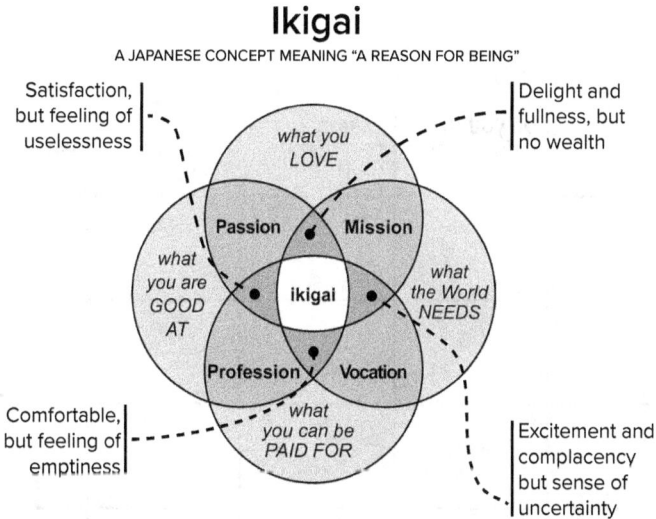

# Ikigai
A JAPANESE CONCEPT MEANING "A REASON FOR BEING"

Satisfaction, but feeling of uselessness

Delight and fullness, but no wealth

what you LOVE

Passion — Mission

what you are GOOD AT — ikigai — what the World NEEDS

Profession — Vocation

Comfortable, but feeling of emptiness

what you can be PAID FOR

Excitement and complacency but sense of uncertainty

Source: https://commons.wikimedia.org/wiki/File: Ikigai-EN.svg

Have a go at putting your ideas for what you might like to do for a career to the above diagram. Where does it fit? How does that make you feel?

What do you think? Is this a useful or illuminating way for you to think about your options?

127

## Exercise

Download the **Understanding yourself Tool (indigo.careers/under standing_apprenticeships)** or create your own table to bring your thoughts together on what you enjoy, what you are good at and whether they are strengths or weaknesses. In the second column say whether you like doing it or not (or whether it's somewhere in between). In the third column, jot down a recent example of when you have done this to make sure you have a concrete instance in mind. Use the fourth column to say how important this particular thing is to you, with 1 as the most important, putting them all in order (this may take several goes). Finally, make sure you do the 'sanity check' in the fifth column to assess whether this is a strength or weakness.

## *Understanding yourself*

|  | Do you like doing this? | Examples (good and bad) | Order of importance for you | Strength or weakness? |
|---|---|---|---|---|
| Spending time with new people |  |  |  |  |
| Organising |  |  |  |  |
| Creativity |  |  |  |  |
| Working with tools |  |  |  |  |
| Solving problems |  |  |  |  |
| Caring for other living things |  |  |  |  |
| Selling & persuading |  |  |  |  |
| Routine vs variety |  |  |  |  |

Add additional rows if there is something else on your mind that you particularly like or dislike that is not included in the list provided.

Jot down your initial thoughts, sleep on it, and then have another look. Discuss it with friends and family members and ask them what they think. They may see things that you do not, and if they agree with you on things, then you can be even more confident in how well you know yourself.

The purpose of this table is to help you think about what you like doing. This won't, by itself, show you directly what careers and apprenticeships are right for you, but it will give you more confidence and insight and mean you are better prepared for whatever apprenticeship you do embark on. No apprenticeship or job in your life will be 'perfect', but if you understand how your preferences, strengths and weaknesses relate to what the job offers, then you will be able to navigate it better and get the most out of it.

# Section 5 summary: Deciding whether to do an apprenticeship

The first thing to realise is that whatever decision you take now is not a decision for life.

But you do have a decision to make on what you are going to do now. You should think about whether you need or want to earn money now, how ready you feel for the adult world and about how clear you are on what you want to do next.

Then think about whether you have the attributes required for an apprenticeship. The most important ones are:

- being interested enough in the occupation and sector
- valuing learning
- being willing and able to take instructions
- being organised (or at least prepared to get organised)
- being resilient (enough).

If you still believe that an apprenticeship is a good path for you, then you need to figure out:

- what is important to you
- what you enjoy doing
- what you are good at
- what your weaknesses are.

Map out your answers and share with others to get their input.

## APPRENTICE CASE STUDY: SOPHIE MAWSON

Sophie studied Physical Education and School Sport at Sheffield Hallam University and graduated with first class honours into the midst of the Covid-19 pandemic. Starting work with her local council, Bradford, to support the council's response to the pandemic she was then recruited into a Covid Support Worker position. Through this she discovered that she really enjoyed helping people and being part of the NHS set up. Her initial ambition to work in schools doing sport was overtaken by her new insight.

She started looking for jobs in the NHS and found one at Health Education England (HEE) as a National Administrator, which was a Level 3 Business Administration apprenticeship. HEE provides the NHS workforce with quality education and training. She recently got promoted and is now a senior programme officer, progressing her career quickly.

'I wasn't actually looking for an apprenticeship – I was looking for a job, but the one that I wanted had the added bonus of the Level 3 qualification.' Even though she had already achieved a degree, she loved the fact that she was getting a professional qualification via the apprenticeship: 'How amazing that I can gain a qualification at the same time as working.'

Her job in the Talent for Care team is, in fact, to support the NHS's own efforts to boost apprenticeships across hospitals and other health trusts. She really enjoys having the opportunity to speak to so many people across the country, helping them set up and develop their apprenticeship programmes.

By her own admission, she does not have a concrete plan for her career: 'This is part of the brilliant thing about my business admin apprenticeship: it gives me such a broad range of skills that I can take to many roles and careers, in the NHS or elsewhere.'

She goes on to highlight how valuable the theory and learning side of her apprenticeship was, rather than just the job by itself: 'I've learned about different types of data, how business finance works and the procurement process, plus much more. The fact that I then get to apply this theory into real life practice in my job makes the learning real.'

She is also critical of how apprenticeships are still perceived by some people: 'There is a stereotype that when you finish your GCSEs, you "should" go on to do A levels and after that you "should" go on to university, and that if you don't, somehow you are stuck or you have failed. This is so wrong. Apprenticeships definitely should not be seen somehow as the "lower" offer.'

She also has some useful advice for people considering their options: 'Take the education path that you want to take, not the one you are being pressured into. You do not have to get a degree to do the career you want to do. An apprenticeship will allow you to test whether you want that career, without any obligation – you're not mentally having to commit yourself like you are when you choose a degree – and you can test that career in practice to see if it's really right for you.'

And for those who are worried about the End Point Assessment at the end of an apprenticeship, she has the following to say: 'I was worried about it, a lot. But in fact, I just had to pick something for End Point Assessment that I had done in my job that I knew I'd done well – in my case, I'd implemented an Action Tracker for our team on a spreadsheet – and walked the person assessing me through it. I'd prepared well and had practised. In the end, it turned out well and I passed.'

So far, Sophie has worked with NHS Trusts across all seven regions in England, helping to support implementation of the 100-plus different apprenticeship standards: so if you end up doing an apprenticeship in the NHS, you may have Sophie to thank!

### EMPLOYER CASE STUDY: TROUP BYWATERS + ANDERS

Troup Bywaters + Anders (TB+A) is a national engineering services consultancy providing advice and support with the design, planning, construction, operation and ongoing management of property and assets in both the public and private sector.

The Partnership had always tried to develop its own people and, like many employers, looked to a graduate scheme as a source of the people they needed. Retention, however, proved to be an issue, and many graduates were slow to record their training and develop to full membership of the professional institutions.

Around 2010, after the financial crash and much talk in the press of the 'Lost Generation', the Partnership decided to start an apprenticeship scheme so that young people could get a start in the industry. TB+A has since built apprenticeships into the heart of its skills development and business model: 20% of their employees are apprentices, and even as the firm has grown, they continue to develop their skills pipeline for the future.

'The icing on the cake is that our clients really love working with our apprentices,' says Neil Weller, who was Managing Partner of the Partnership from 2005 to 2016. 'The whole programme is core to our continued business success.'

The fundamental reason, Neil goes on to say, for this success is the way in which apprentices learn. 'Building Services Engineering is not something you are able to learn just at college or university. Learning needs to be equally done in the workplace with experienced engineers. Things like low energy, sustainability, ESG, fire safety and many other things change on a year-by-year basis, sometimes on a month-by-month basis. It is unlikely training providers or lecturers can necessarily keep up. It needs to be a joint effort.'

The way in which an apprenticeship works, Neil says, means that there is a powerful learning blend of three things: 1) the academic knowledge 2) the latest approaches and techniques being deployed by experienced and commercial managers and 3) the practical hands-on application of skills in day-to-day work. 'Apprentices are working day to day with people who can really train them on what matters. They can make mistakes, but people are there to nurture them and guide them.'

He goes on to note how much apprenticeships have improved in the last ten years: 'We have been involved in the creation of new Apprenticeship Standards for the whole sector, and we know that we are getting better and better at creating apprenticeship programmes that really work.'

# Section 6
# Finding a good apprenticeship to apply for

# Introduction to Section 6: Finding a good apprenticeship to apply for

The next two sections are all about helping you to find an apprenticeship that's right for you.

Section 6 covers:

- geography: you need to be able to physically get to an apprenticeship from where you live
- the kind of apprenticeships to apply for
- how to find apprenticeship opportunities, online and offline.

Section 7 then looks at how to apply for and get the apprenticeships that most interest you.

# 6.1 Geography: which employers can you physically get to?

The reality is that the jobs market in the UK is not evenly spread around the country. For example, large-scale manufacturing and engineering firms typically cluster in a few regions of the country, such as advanced automotive engineering in the south Midlands. And there are only 11 nuclear sites in the whole of the UK, so if you want to be a nuclear engineering apprentice then you have to be able to get to one of them.

Media jobs are typically in the larger cities, like Manchester and London. Banking and legal services follow a similar pattern. And where cities are large and economically successful, like London, there tend to be lots of different kinds of jobs and therefore apprenticeships.

Other employers are much more widespread: Network Rail operates all over the country, as do organisations like BT as well as councils and NHS organisations. But even for jobs that are to be found in all parts of the country, like public sector jobs (NHS and other healthcare, local government), retail, leisure and hospitality, etc., there will be different patterns of whether apprenticeships are available and in what numbers.

And of course, it's not just the employers offering apprenticeships – there also needs to be a training provider who delivers in the location where you want to do your apprenticeship.

Finally, there is the rather prosaic but important question about travel arrangements. You may have found your dream apprenticeship, but if it's going to take three buses, one train and a long walk to get there you may find, despite your early enthusiasm, that it is just not realistic to sustain such a lengthy commute.

There are some apprenticeships where the employer may offer relocation packages. Even if the employer you want to do an apprenticeship with does not, it's still worth considering whether you are prepared to move in order to take up an apprenticeship. Some apprentices move into house shares with other apprentices from the same company or live with a relative or family friend who lives within commuting distance of the employer. Stay creative and explore your options.

# 6.2 What apprenticeships should you consider?

Keep in mind your answers to all your questions about yourself from Section 5, and start to relate those to the apprenticeships you are looking at.

With those in mind, identify different options for apprenticeships by asking yourself three questions.

1. What 'occupation' do you want to start your career in?
2. What 'sector' do you want to work in?
3. And what kind of 'organisation' do you want to work for?

Let's look at each of these in turn:

## 1. Occupation: What do you want to be?

In the modern economy there are many different occupations, which is why there are so many apprenticeships (more than 600 at the time of writing this book); everything from being a butcher, a doctor or a digital marketer to the more 'traditional' apprenticeship occupations such as being a plumber or electrician.

If you want to see the full list for yourself, go to the Institute for Apprenticeships and Technical Education's website, institutefor apprenticeships.org/apprenticeship-standards and have an explore.

On the following pages is a table of the main occupational 'groups' of apprenticeships available.

## *Main occupational groups of apprenticeships*

| Apprenticeship category according to IfATE | Number of Apprenticeship Standards approved or in development | Description | Examples of Apprenticeship Standards |
|---|---|---|---|
| Agriculture, environmental and animal care | 43 | Usually outdoors, often working with and tending animals, plants and outdoor spaces | Animal trainer, Forest operative, Equine groom, Golf greenkeeper, Veterinary nurse |
| Business and administration | 45 | Normally office-based, supporting the everyday workings of an office | HR support, Associate project manager, Junior management consultant, Corporate responsibility and sustainability practitioner |
| Care services | 15 | Working with people who need help and support, such as children, young people or adults with additional needs, the elderly | Playworker, Youth worker, Social worker, Adult care worker |
| Catering and hospitality | 12 | Cooking in kitchens and restaurants, running hospitality venues such as pubs | Production chef, Pastry chef, Hospitality team member, Hospitality supervisor |
| Construction and the built environment | 106 | Building and maintaining the buildings and physical infrastructure that we all depend on; lots of physical and outdoor work and/or on and in construction sites; often a 'hard hat' role; often using specialist tools and equipment | Electrician, Telecoms installer, Plasterer, Roofer, Facilities management, Steelwork fabricator, Bricklayer, Painter and decorator, Carpentry and joinery, Plumbing and domestic heating, Highways maintenance, Smart meter installer |

| Apprenticeship category according to IfATE | Number of Apprenticeship Standards approved or in development | Description | Examples of Apprenticeship Standards |
|---|---|---|---|
| Creative and design | 68 | Creating and designing new things for people to experience and enjoy, in theatre and concert venues, television, radio, print and museums and galleries | Scenic Artist, Audiovisual Technician, Camera Prep Technician, Junior Advertising Creative, Jeweller, Silversmith, Museums and Galleries technician, Live event technician, Publishing assistant |
| Digital | 31 | Designing, creating, maintaining and using digital and data technology infrastructure for organisations | Information communications technician, IT solutions technician, Cyber security technologist, Data technician, Data analyst, DevOps engineer, Business analyst, Software development technician |
| Education and early years | 12 | Working with children and adults who are in education | Early years practitioner, Teaching assistant, Teacher, Learning and Skills assessor |

| Apprenticeship category according to IfATE | Number of Apprenticeship Standards approved or in development | Description | Examples of Apprenticeship Standards |
|---|---|---|---|
| Engineering and manufacturing | 169 | Manufacturing, installing and maintaining the crucial components in the physical assets and infrastructure of all of our lives; often outdoors or in industrial settings; often 'hard hat' roles that also have office time | Water industry treatment process technician, Engineer surveyor, Space engineering technician, Window fabricator, Pipe welder, Wood product manufacturing operative, Vehicle damage technician, Metal fabricator, Engineering fitter, Motorcycle technician, Bicycle mechanic, Engineering operative, Nuclear operative, Marine engineer, General welder, Rail engineering operative, Boatbuilder, Utilities engineering technician |
| Hair and beauty | 9 | Helping people to look good and feel confident | Beauty therapist, Hair professional, Wellbeing and holistic therapist |
| Health and science | 88 | Keeping people healthy through direct medical care and support and scientific research | Doctor, Sports coach, Pharmacy technician, Oral health practitioner, Dental nurse, Dietitian, Sonographer, Nurse, Physiotherapist |
| Legal, finance and accounting | 43 | Helping organisations to ensure their dealings are legal, well managed and commercially successful | Accountant, Insurance practitioner, Paralegal, Solicitor, Payroll administrator, Compliance and risk officer, Credit Controller, Investment operations, Financial Services administrator |

| Apprenticeship category according to IfATE | Number of Apprenticeship Standards approved or in development | Description | Examples of Apprenticeship Standards |
|---|---|---|---|
| Protective services | 20 | Keeping people safe | Fire safety Inspector, Community safety advisor, Police Community support officer, Police constable, Firefighter, Security first line manager |
| Sales, marketing and procurement | 37 | Helping organisations to sell their products and services to others, helping organisations to buy products and services from others | Market researcher, Procurement and supply assistant, Fundraiser, Marketing assistant, Advertising and media executive, Sales executive, Junior estate agent, Public relations and communications assistant, Event assistant, Travel consultant, Retailer, Digital marketer, Housing and property management assistant |
| Transport and logistics | 40 | Operating and processing vehicles (of all kinds) and looking after passengers | Rail infrastructure operator, Port agent, Urban driver, Aviation customer service operative, Transport and warehouse operations supervisor, Boatmaster, Train driver, Cabin crew, Passenger transport operative, LGV driver |

*A quick note: For more information on apprenticeships available in Scotland, Wales and Northern Ireland, go to:*

- *apprenticeships.scot*
- *careerswales.gov.wales/apprenticeships*
- *nidirect.gov.uk/campaigns/apprenticeships.*

If you are focused on doing an apprenticeship that will develop or use your 'green skills' – the kind of skills that are going to be needed to enable us to mitigate the impacts of climate change – there is a specific filter on the IfATE's website to find these roles in particular.

There are two important things to note when thinking about 'occupation'.

First, what you do for the first few years of your career does not mean you are going to have to do that for the rest of your life. There is an increasing phenomenon of people having multiple careers during their working life. While for some people, picking one occupation and becoming truly expert over a long period is the right thing, for others, changing and trying out different careers is the right thing.

Secondly, the world, the economy and therefore the occupations in it have never been changing faster, so there are occupations that are going to be huge in five years' time that may not even have a name yet. Whatever you think is a good choice for you now, remember that it does not have to be for life and could be overtaken by economic developments anyway.

If you're not sure about what occupations you are interested in, to get started go through the list above and identify two or three categories from the first column. Then go to the IfATE website (instituteforapprenticeships.org) and search on apprenticeship standards – or have a look at the occupational maps. Then identify three or four apprenticeship standards that catch your eye and read through them in a bit more detail. In this way you will start to get a sense of what appeals to you, and why.

Use the table opposite from the **Narrowing down your apprenticeship Tool (also available to download at indigo.careers/understanding_ apprenticeships**) to think about the different occupational areas you might be interested in. Use the Institute for Apprenticeship's website (instituteforapprenticeships.org) to identify which apprenticeship standards are of interest to you, remembering to check that the level is appropriate for you.

## Narrowing down your apprenticeship – occupation

| Occupational area | How much does this area interest you? (Score 1 to 5, with 1 being 'of no interest' and 5 being 'of significant interest' | Specific apprenticeship standards of interest | Your reasons for being interested | What more you want to find out |
|---|---|---|---|---|
| Agriculture, environmental and animal care | | | | |
| Business and administration | | | | |
| Care services | | | | |
| Catering and hospitality | | | | |
| Construction and the built environment | | | | |
| Creative and design | | | | |
| Digital | | | | |
| Education and early years | | | | |
| Engineering and manufacturing | | | | |
| Hair and beauty | | | | |
| Health and science | | | | |
| Legal, finance and accounting | | | | |
| Protective services | | | | |
| Sales, marketing and procurement | | | | |
| Transport and logistics | | | | |

## 2. What sector do you want to work in?

Having explored which occupation you might be interested in, now let's look at 'sector'.

A sector is an area of the economy that produces a category of product or service. Examples include retail and wholesale, health and social care, manufacturing, construction, IT and communications, and financial services (among quite a few others). Within sectors there are sub-sectors, so within health and social care are sub-sectors like hospitals, pharmacies, care homes, etc.

You may be motivated primarily by working in a specific sector without being clear at this stage what occupation you want in that sector. For example, you may want to work in entertainment, financial services or healthcare. If this is how you are motivated, the challenge for you is that apprenticeships are not built around sectors, but around occupations. So you still have to identify an occupation (or occupations) to apply for, even if you do not really mind that much. As with other decisions you make around apprenticeships, remember that what you do now is not for life: there are many people who started their career in their chosen sector in one occupation and then, having established themselves, switch to a different occupation in the same sector that then becomes their career.

Some occupations are only found in specific sectors; for example, you can only really be a doctor in the healthcare sector or an investment administrator in the finance industry. But there are occupations that can be found in lots of different sectors; for example, if you want to be an accountant or a data analyst, then you could end up working in pretty much any sector (all organisations need accounts and use data after all). So you may find that having decided on an occupation, you still need to consider which sector you may enjoy working in.

Be guided by what you are interested in and where you feel you will be motivated by the core purpose of the sector. If you find yourself not caring that much about which sector you want to work in, that's fine! But it's definitely worth thinking about.

Use the second table in the **Narrowing down your apprenticeship Tool (also available to download at indigo.careers/understanding_ apprenticeships)** on the following page to explore particular sectors that appeal to you.

## *Narrowing down your apprenticeship – sector*

| Industrial sector | Examples | How much does this sector interest you? (Score 1 to 5, with 1 being 'of no interest' and 5 being 'of significant interest') | Your reasons for being interested | What more you want to find out |
|---|---|---|---|---|
| Retail and wholesale | *shop, shopping website* | | | |
| Health and social care | *hospital, care provider* | | | |
| Professional and technical | *accountancy firm* | | | |
| Administration and support | *outsourcing company* | | | |
| Education | *school or college* | | | |
| Manufacturing | *car production, precision engineers* | | | |
| Catering and hospitality | *hotel, restaurant* | | | |
| Construction | *building firm* | | | |
| Transport | *rail company* | | | |
| Public sector and defence | *local government, army* | | | |
| IT and communications | *mobile phone company, IT business* | | | |
| Financial services | *bank, insurance firm* | | | |
| Arts, entertainment and recreation | *gallery, film production* | | | |
| Other services | *advertising* | | | |
| Real estate activities | *estate agent, property manager* | | | |
| Utilities | *electricity company* | | | |
| Agriculture | *farm* | | | |

> ## 💡 Interesting idea: The zigzag career
>
> Careers are often described as though they happen in a 'straight line', with one step logically leading to the next. This career model is based on the 20th-century economy, when it was common for people to work their whole life for just one employer or to have made logical steps up a predictable career ladder.
>
> Neither of these scenarios is often the case now. Far more common is the 'zigzag' career, in which someone's next job may look very different to the one that came before or the one that will come after. Normally, but not always, there will be some sort of connection between the jobs – but it won't be just about getting the next most senior job title or a simple pay rise.
>
> There are two other concepts now challenging the idea of 'one' career: these are the 'portfolio career' and the '100-Year Life'.
>
> A portfolio career describes someone's work life who does multiple different things at the same time. I have a portfolio career: as well as writing this guidebook, I do consulting work for different organisations and I am also a personal trainer. Many people, starting in their teens and twenties are developing portfolio careers, often with business side hustles alongside their paid, 'regular' job.
>
> Of course, it is hard to undertake an apprenticeship successfully as part of a portfolio career, because of the demands on your time, energy and attention to maintain both the work and learning parts of an apprenticeship. But it may make sense to undertake an apprenticeship as part of a strategy to create a portfolio career.
>
> The 100-Year Life is a concept developed by Lynda Gratton of the London Business School; it is based on the fact that we are all living longer, which in turn opens up the possibilities of having two, maybe three, separate careers, one after the other. Again, there would be nothing to stop you doing an apprenticeship in one area, continuing with that occupation for 10–15 years, and then starting all over again in a totally different one.
>
> Parents, teachers and friends may talk as though whatever you decide to do now will set you on your 'forever' career path. The reality in the 21st century, as jobs and whole occupations come and go with increasing rapidity, is that the zigzag career is far more likely to be the 'norm' than a 'job for life'.

## 3. Type of organisation

Having thought about occupation and sector, you should also think about which type of 'organisation' you might want to work for.

Big organisations are typically more stable. The pros are that they are more likely to have supporting processes and people in place, there will be more structure for your apprenticeship (both the job and the learning) and there will be more people to learn from and for your network; the 'cons' are that they may be slower moving and it may be harder to forge an identity for yourself in the organisation.

Small organisations can give you more exposure to more things more quickly – but this is likely to be more up and down both as the organisation itself goes up and down and as the availability and support of people around you will sometimes be in short supply. As a rule of thumb, the smaller the organisation the more like a roller coaster it will be. Some people like roller coasters, some people don't, and that's fine – but have a think about what you will like.

You might think that a medium-sized organisation could provide the best of both worlds: stability and opportunity. This can be true, but it might also be the worst of both worlds – not very stable and with few opportunities! You can only find this out by researching potential employers thoroughly.

Anthony Impey, Chief Executive of Be The Business, the UK's national productivity improvement initiative, has an interesting point of view on what kind of organisation you might want to look at for your apprenticeship: 'The last three years have seen some massive shocks to every type of business – from lockdowns to inflation. It's been difficult for many, but the more entrepreneurial ones have been able to turn these challenges into new opportunities. Smaller, more nimble businesses are going to continue to thrive in the years ahead and offer some of the most exciting career opportunities. So, you shouldn't think that the 'best' apprenticeships are always going to be with the big firms you've heard of. With small and medium-sized firms you'll be closer to all the different parts of the organisation, meaning you're more likely to learn more, progress faster, and hone your entrepreneurial skills. Smaller can be better and might get you the very best start to your career.'

You should also think about whether you want to work for a for-profit enterprise (a business), a government organisation, such as a council or civil service department, or a non-profit (a charity). Of course, within most of these organisations, regardless of whether they are private sector, government or non-profit, there are going to be many different types of teams you could join, and many different types of roles.

Use the third table in the **Narrowing down your apprenticeship Tool (also available to download at indigo.careers/understanding_ apprenticeships)** to help you structure your thinking about what apprenticeships you might be interested in. If you do not have any particular preference, that's fine (but it's worth asking yourself the question!).

## Narrowing down your apprenticeship – organisation

| Size | Tick to indicate your preference(s) (if you have one) | What are your reasons? |
|---|---|---|
| Micro (10 or less employees) | | |
| Small and Medium (10–250 employees) | | |
| Large (250–5,000 employees) | | |
| Macro (5,000 or more employees) | | |
| Dynamics | Tick to indicate your preference(s) (if you have one) | What are your reasons? |
| Fast growth | | |
| Stable | | |
| Type | Tick to indicate your preference(s) (if you have one) | What are your reasons? |
| Private sector/ commercial/for profit | | |
| Independent not-for-profit (e.g. charity) | | |
| Public sector | | |

## 💡 Interesting idea: The most common apprenticeships

The most common apprenticeship standards for 16–18-year-olds in 2021/22 were:

- Business Administrator, Level 3
- Hair Professional, Level 2
- Installation Electrician and Maintenance Electrician, Level 3
- Early Years Practitioner, Level 2
- Carpentry and Joinery, Level 2
- Early Years Educator, Level 3
- Engineering Technician, Level 3
- Customer Service Practitioner, Level 2
- Plumbing and Domestic Heating Technician, Level 3
- Bricklayer, Level 2
- Motor Vehicle Service and Maintenance Technician (Light Vehicle), Level 3
- Dental Nurse, Level 3
- Hospitality Team Member, Level 2
- HM Forces Serviceperson (Public Services), Level 2
- Teaching Assistant, Level 3
- Assistant Accountant, Level 3
- Autocare Technician, Level 2

And for those aged 19–23 in 2021/22 were:

- Accountancy or Taxation Professional, Level 7 Degree Apprenticeship
- Business Administrator, Level 3
- Early Years Educator, Level 3
- Engineering Technician, Level 3
- Police Constable, Level 6 Degree Apprenticeship
- Installation Electrician and Maintenance Electrician, Level 3
- Adult Care Worker, Level 2
- Lead Adult Care Worker, Level 3
- Information Communications Technician, Level 3
- HM Forces Serviceperson (Public Services), Level 2
- Team Leader or Supervisor, Level 3
- Customer Service Practitioner, Level 3
- Digital Marketer, Level 3
- Dental Nurse, Level 3
- Professional Accounting or Taxation Technician, Level 7
- Early Years Practitioner, Level 2
- Assistant Accountant, Level 3

# 6.3 How to find apprenticeships to apply for

## Overview

By now you should have the following things a little clearer in your mind:

- Whether an apprenticeship could be a good option for you as your next step (and why).
- What you want to do with your career (what is important to you and what you enjoy and are good at).
- What occupations and sectors you are interested in, and what kind of organisation appeals to you most.

This means you are now ready to start looking for specific apprenticeships to apply for.

The good news is, it has never been easier to apply for an apprenticeship – and it is getting easier as apprenticeships become more and more established.

To maximise your chances of success and minimise the stress involved you will need to develop a clear plan and strategy for how you will find your apprenticeship.

The key things to think about are the following.

1. How many apprenticeships to apply for.
2. Organising your applications.
3. Your 'sources' (where are you going to look).

## 1. How many apprenticeships to apply for

You sometimes hear heart-breaking stories about people who have applied for hundreds of jobs and yet have been rejected, sometimes without getting an interview, from every single one.

Whenever I hear these, I am upset, not because of their bad luck but because no one has pointed out to them that the reason they have not succeeded is **because** they have applied for hundreds of jobs.

Let me explain: to write a good covering letter and to tailor a CV for a particular role takes at least an hour, even when you have become quite good at the process. If someone is applying for hundreds of jobs, unless they are spending hundreds of hours on the process, it is unlikely that the applications will be very good: it is not surprising that they are not succeeding.

On the other hand, applying for too few apprenticeships is also a sub-optimal strategy. This is for a few reasons.

First, until you go to meet an organisation you just don't know what the opportunity is really like – it might not be what you hoped it would be. Second, it is good for your confidence while you are going through one application process to know that not everything depends on just this one opportunity; this confidence, ironically, will probably make you more likely to do well! And, finally, going through multiple application processes will enable you to learn more and more quickly than if you stake everything just on one or two opportunities. I would recommend applying for at least five but no more than ten in the first instance.

However, there are people who set their sights on just one and completely go for it (the case study of Janelle Raphahane is a good example, see page 15). There are advantages to having laser-like focus and determination (especially if this can shine through to the prospective employer), but it is a higher risk strategy.

It is quite possible that you are unsuccessful in this first 'round' of five to ten apprenticeship applications, so be prepared to continue applying, but I would suggest you do so in small 'batches' of three to five apprenticeships in order to stay focused and maintain the quality of your applications.

Do not take rejections personally: remember that an employer assessing you is having to make a decision with very limited information about you – they do not really know you at all. There will be at least one employer out there who will love you – you just have to 'play the numbers game', be patient and keep on applying with positivity and determination.

## 2. Organising your applications

Set up a system to help track and manage your apprenticeship applications.

The Find An Apprenticeship service (gov.uk/apply-apprenticeship) has some functionality to store the applications that you make through the site (and if you find an apprenticeship through UCAS, it will typically direct you to the Find An Apprenticeship service site too). However, there may be some details that you will want to track yourself and, of course, you may want to apply for apprenticeships through different routes.

Depending on how many apprenticeships you apply for, it is worth thinking about how you best manage this. You might want to set up a table or spreadsheet to help you to do this, perhaps looking a bit like the table below (also available to download, see the **Managing apprenticeship applications Tool** at **indigo.careers/understanding_apprenticeships**).

The black shaded columns are the purely descriptive details. The first column is where you can record the name of the job (you can either use the one used by the employer or your own description – you might also want to include any hyperlinks to the original online source if there is one). Then record what the employer, salary and apprenticeship standard is.

The grey shaded columns are your action columns. In the first column, record where you are up to, for example 'submitted application',

## *Managing apprenticeship applications*

| Job title | Employer | Salary | Apprentice-ship standard | Stage you are at | Your next action |
|-----------|----------|--------|--------------------------|------------------|------------------|
|           |          |        |                          |                  |                  |
|           |          |        |                          |                  |                  |
|           |          |        |                          |                  |                  |

'arranged first interview', 'been invited to assessment centre'. Obviously, this is a column you will update and change as the process develops. So too will the next column, where you should keep track of what you should do next, e.g. 'prepare questions for interview', 'further research the company before assessment centre', 'check on dress code for interview'. The next column is for you to keep a note of any important contact details, perhaps a key person at the organisation or at the training provider.

Finally, the non-shaded columns are your evaluation columns. Use these columns to score each opportunity, using your best judgement. You could score out of 5, with 1 being the worst and 5 being the best. Make sure you use the same scale consistently, and that your score fits your overall judgement. Think back to all the research you have done, but ultimately trust your intuitions.

- Score how easy it will be for you to get to the workplace of that employer.
- Reach a view on how well the apprenticeship opportunity fits with your overall aspirations, with what you enjoy and your strengths and weaknesses.
- Assess your views of the employer.
- Assess your views of the training provider.

Finally, say where this fits in your overall ranking of apprenticeship opportunities, with 1 as your favourite apprenticeship. This is likely to change as you add and remove apprenticeship opportunities from the table.

| Important contact details | Travel time/ ease | How well it hits your goals, what you enjoy/ strengths | Employer evaluation | Training provider evaluation | Your overall ranking |
|---|---|---|---|---|---|
| | | | | | |
| | | | | | |
| | | | | | |

Keeping a single record of the apprenticeships that you are interested in will enable you to keep track of your applications, stay on top of the admin and keep an 'always developing' sense of what your preferences are. It means you can share your thinking with other people, and it will prompt you to do further research and ask the right questions.

Remember, at any one time there may not be many (or even any!) apprenticeships available within your geographic range – or indeed, anywhere in the country. This is especially true if the apprenticeship is highly specialist or unusual. In these cases, come back to check with the websites you are using to find apprenticeships on a regular basis (and definitely sign up for automated alerts if available). Perhaps set aside a particular time once a week to check in on the website to see if any new apprenticeships have come up.

## 3. Where to look online...

There are two official websites – the Government's main apprenticeship site and UCAS – and a number of others worth registering with.

The Government's main website for finding an apprenticeship is gov. uk/apply-apprenticeship. While it isn't mandatory to advertise here, Government strongly encourages training providers and employers to use it.

You will need to create an account and sign up for the alert settings you want (e.g. what you want alerts for, whether by email or text, etc.).

Once you have done that, you can click on 'find an apprenticeship' and get going with your search. You can put in a job title, an employer name or a reference number (for example, if you have seen it advertised somewhere else but want to check on it here). You can specify whether you are looking for employers who are disability confident too.

You can also set how far away from your home address you want to consider any apprenticeship. My advice on this is to go further than you think – after all, your transport options are not determined necessarily by how far somewhere is from your home address, but, for example, by what public transport links are like or where you might be able to get a lift to.

The other official online source is the UCAS website (ucas.com) which, since 2023, includes a growing number of apprenticeship opportunities. You may well already have a UCAS account if you have applied for further or higher education courses. From the home page just click on 'apprenticeships' or search using the main search function and you will find your way to 'career finder' where you can find apprenticeships.

Because UCAS has only just started hosting apprenticeship opportunities, it is not (yet) as comprehensive as the government's Find an Apprenticeship site. But there are more and more opportunities there every month.

In both cases, the search functionality is not perfect, so you need to be prepared to be patient and diligent as you search.

As well as the 'official' websites, there are a number of other websites where you will find not only apprenticeship opportunities but also advice and guidance. Remember, most of these websites need to generate revenue to keep themselves going, which means they will take payment from employers for advertising particular apprenticeships. This is not such a bad thing – if an employer is willing to pay extra to advertise their opportunity then they are probably even more keen to find people for it! But it does mean that they are not completely objective and you may find that some employers and apprenticeships get more prominence than would be 'fair'.

These include (but are not limited to):

- amazingapprenticeships.com
- getmyfirstjob.co.uk
- allaboutcareers.com
- notgoingtouni.co.uk
- apprenticeshipguide.co.uk (this is produced in partnership with the Department for Education's National Apprenticeship Service, and is 'semi'-official).

Have a look at each of these, find which ones you like and sign up for accounts and the alerts you want. You may find the same apprenticeship opportunities popping up on more than one of these sites. Experiment and find out which ones work best for you. Take advantage of the advice and guidance they have to offer.

If you want to throw the net even wider, then you can go to general jobs websites, such as jobsgopublic.com, uk.indeed.com, jobs.theguardian.com and linkedin.com.

> ## 💡 Interesting idea: Your LinkedIn profile
>
> LinkedIn is a global professional and business networking site. There were nearly 35 million(!) members in the UK alone in December 2022 – it is extremely likely that whoever will be hiring you, including the people interviewing you, will be on LinkedIn.
>
> Having a profile on LinkedIn signals to potential employers that you are 'in' the world of work and ready to see, be seen and take advantage of the networking and research possibilities that the platform brings.
>
> If you have already done your CV, then completing a LinkedIn profile will be easy to do. It is also a free platform.
>
> Once you have a profile, you can do the following.
>
> - Start to follow people who you think will be interesting and who you can learn from (from the famous, like Stephen Bartlett and Bill Gates, to people who are recognised influencers in their field).
> - Join groups that are themed on either the occupations or sectors you are interested in.
> - Get recommendations from people who have worked with you.
> - Engage with posts to generate similar posts in your timeline.
> - Start to post yourself and maybe even write an article to show off your interest – do not worry about how original or brilliant you are, just getting started will be valuable.
>
> You can share your profile as part of your applications, and people viewing it will see all of your activity as well. It's a great way to 'show off' what you are about and to impress potential employers.

## ... & offline

According to HubSpot, the global marketing platform, 85% of jobs are filled through networking, i.e. through personal connections. This is a vital source of potential roles too.

Talk to people you know: older siblings, cousins, uncles, aunts, your neighbours and people you know in your community or area.

Do not be shy: people love to help out young people, and really like to be asked. Ask them if they can give you work experience, if not an apprenticeship. Even if they can't, they will remember that you are looking and mention it to their friends who may have opportunities. The more you talk, positively and politely, about what you want to do, the more chance you have of 'getting lucky'.

Even if they cannot guide you to any specific opportunities, you will learn all sorts of useful things just by talking to others. Ask them about their job: what they do on a typical day, what they like about it, what they would change about it and how they think you would enjoy it.

And remember, just because you've asked them once doesn't mean you can't ask them again when you've done some more research (in fact, people will love the fact that you have come back to them for more advice).

# 6.4 How to evaluate employers and training providers

Your employer and your training provider will play a huge role in your apprenticeship. It is important that for every apprenticeship you apply for you have done your research on both these organisations.

## Researching a potential employer
*Why is it important that you research the potential employer?*

It is important that the organisation who employs you and who will support you through your apprenticeship is a good one for your aspirations and your needs.

A healthy and successful organisation will be more able to invest in you and give you the time and support that you need than one that is struggling. It will also be more likely to have the internal structures and disciplines that will enable you to learn and flourish.

In addition, you should try to find a company that aligns with your values. If it feels like 'your kind of place', where you believe and trust in the intentions of the people around you and if they are the kind of people that you will enjoy being with for eight or more hours a day, then you will have a more enjoyable and satisfying apprenticeship.

*How can you find all of this out?*

Begin by looking at their website. Look beyond the home page to see if you can find out how the organisation operates and how its people think and act. If you are able to identify senior managers from the website, you could search for them on LinkedIn where you will see how they present themselves to their fellow professional community. They might say on the careers part of the corporate website that they are passionate about developing young talent – but is that what they also say to their network on LinkedIn?

Act like a customer and search for customer reviews of the organisation's products and services. Search for the employer online and see what comes up, especially under the 'news' search function. You are looking to find out if they are good at what they do, liked by their customers/users and also to see if there are any clues as to how financially stable and successful they are.

You can also look on Glassdoor (glassdoor.co.uk) to see what current and previous employees think. Also go to ratemyapprenticeship.co.uk/best-apprenticeship-employers to see if you can find out specifically how different employers are assessed by real apprentices.

Of course, you need to treat these reviews with a pinch of salt: every organisation will have disgruntled customers and ex-employees, but you should be able to get a good impression of whether it's a flourishing organisation or one that's struggling. Find the organisation's profile on LinkedIn and see what its posts are like. Do the same on its other social media channels. Do you like what you see?

All of this research will be gold dust should you decide to apply and get to an interview – you'll know lots about them and have loads of questions to ask!

## Researching a training provider

While your employer is the most important organisation for your apprenticeship, your training provider will also play a key role, ensuring you formally complete all aspects of the apprenticeship qualification. So it is worth researching them to spot any red flags, to identify key questions you want to ask them and to be as prepared as you can be. Remember, your training provider can either be a Further Education college, an Independent Training Provider or the employer themselves.

You can begin with any Ofsted inspections they may have had at reports.ofsted.gov.uk. There are four possible ratings a training provider can get (just like a school or college): Outstanding, Good, Requires Improvement or Inadequate. If a provider is 'inadequate' then it is unlikely to be taking on any new apprentices. If it 'requires improvement' then dig into the report to find out what the issues were – and don't be afraid to ask the training provider what they have done to address those issues since they had their inspection.

The key thing with Ofsted grades is to look at when the inspection was. If it is any more than a couple of years old then take it with a pinch of salt (whether it is good or bad). Things can change very quickly for a training provider, which means that someone who was 'outstanding' a few years ago – and according to Ofsted still is – may have gone through some wobbles; and a training provider who a few years ago was deemed as 'requires improvement' may now be delivering brilliant apprenticeships.

Do general searches online to see if you can get any further insight, perhaps focusing in on 'news' results. Try to contact people who have used that training provider themselves to find out what you can expect, where their strengths are and what their weaknesses are.

Remember that every apprenticeship provider will have apprentices who are real fans (because their apprenticeship has worked out well) and apprentices who are really unhappy with them (because their apprenticeship has not worked out well). In both cases, it may not always be because of the training provider!

## 💡 Interesting idea: 'What if I can't find any apprenticeships that I want?'

You have done your self-reflection. You have carefully researched careers that sound right for you. You have concluded that a particular apprenticeship, or a small sub-set of apprenticeships, looks like a good option for you.

You have then done your online and offline research but discovered that there do not appear to be any of these apprenticeships available! Do not despair!

Here are some considerations and suggested steps:

● Identify the kind of organisations that you wish were offering the apprenticeships you want. Get in touch with them and ask to speak to whoever is in charge of hiring people. Ask them how they hire people and if they have ever considered apprenticeships – maybe this is the nudge they need! If they do not use apprenticeships but have other pathways into employment then you should consider these (remember, getting a 'regular' job, volunteering and/or while completing non-apprenticeship qualifications are good options too).

● Remember that your apprenticeship is about getting started on your career, not about defining what you do forever. Is there another apprenticeship (or apprenticeships) that are available that are similar to what you want to do?

● It may be that the apprenticeships do exist but are not available right now: buy time by getting a short-term job so you are active and earning money, while continuing to research hard for the right opportunity.

● It may be that you have to take a sideways move first, into an apprenticeship and career that may not be your first choice.

◆ As is the case with some of the case studies in this book, it may be that your second choice turns out to be better than the one you thought you wanted.

◆ Once you have got started in your career, you will be well placed to make the move into the career you originally wanted (either as an apprentice or into a non-apprenticeship job) – remember the zigzag career!

● Re-consider university, particularly if there are good enough courses at good enough universities for the career you are interested in (but beware defaulting to uni because it is seen as a good thing to do – make sure it really is for you).

# Section 6 summary: Finding a good apprenticeship to apply for

Keep in mind what you know about yourself (from Section 5).

Whatever catches your eye needs to be physically accessible – where you live or are prepared to live is a factor that you cannot ignore.

You need to think about:

- what 'occupation' you want to start your career in, e.g. do you want to be a data analyst, hospitality manager, electrician or engineer?
- the 'sector' you want to be part of, e.g. the health, finance or manufacturing sector (occupation and sector often overlap, but not always)
- the kind of organisation you want to work for, e.g. private or government, large or small.

When you have some initial answers to these questions, begin your search. Do not try to apply for too many apprenticeships – but you should apply for more than one. Make sure you are able to organise and keep track of your applications.

Look at the two main 'official' websites for apprenticeship opportunities: the Government's 'Find an Apprenticeship' service and UCAS But also look at other websites – there are lots out there. And do not forget to look offline too – word of mouth is still an important way to find out about opportunities.

Create a system through which you can then systematically evaluate the different apprenticeships you find, to make sure you concentrate on applying for the ones that most closely match your aspirations. Research potential employers and training providers carefully.

### APPRENTICE CASE STUDY: TOM BALLARD

Tom is currently a Principal Web Developer at design agency AKQA, working on web projects promoting some of the world's most famous brands. He started his apprenticeship in web development back in 2014.

'I love my role. It's great to be able to see something so tangible as the output from my work – and to know that thousands (maybe hundreds of thousands) of people are seeing it as well. It's exciting.' As someone who benefited significantly from managers who helped him to develop his skills, he also now enjoys helping junior developers to improve and hone their skills.

Tom's route through his apprenticeship was not simple because of chronic health issues, which first became apparent during his A levels. 'I was worried about locking myself into a three-year commitment on a university course which could be affected by my health condition – an apprenticeship for just over a year felt more flexible.'

And, indeed, during Tom's apprenticeship, his health issues became sufficiently serious that he had to take an extended break to resolve them – and then had to switch jobs to reduce his travel time. The fact that he was able to do all of this, he says, was in large part because of the structure of an apprenticeship.

One other interesting point that Tom makes is that he got important advice even before he had begun his apprenticeship: he was applying for a social media apprenticeship with the company that became his first employer, but at interview they told him they thought he would be better suited to a web development apprenticeship they were recruiting for at the same time. 'I wouldn't have got that kind of advice and steer from a university. Without that, I wouldn't be where I am today.'

He also has this advice for those with a chronic health condition who worry it will affect whether they can successfully apply for and complete an apprenticeship: 'Go for it. Good employers will always be more interested in what you can do and in your skills, and will be willing to help you.' He makes the good point that many people with chronic health issues are probably pretty used to overcoming difficulties – and that's a good trait to be able to show employers.

Finally, Tom has relevant advice to anyone comparing an apprenticeship to a university course in a discipline that is changing rapidly (like web development): what you learn in a 15-month apprenticeship will, by definition, be relevant to the workplace (because you've been learning it in the workplace) – whereas what you learn on a three-year university course might be irrelevant by the time you get to the workplace, and universities do not always know what the workplace really needs.

## EMPLOYER CASE STUDY: MCDONALD'S

McDonald's UK & Ireland has been offering apprenticeships since 2006, supporting over 19,500 people with their professional development. They know that apprenticeships support both individuals and the business, and are a fantastic way for their people to gain a nationally recognised qualification, to progress in their business and to develop knowledge, skills and confidence.

As Ilona Hodson, McDonald's National Apprenticeship Manager says, 'Apprenticeships are a key tool at McDonald's to increase attraction and retention and boost talent pipelines that help create a skilled workforce for us for the future.'

One of the key benefits for offering apprenticeships is that they provide vocational training opportunities for people who might not respond as well to more traditional education routes. 'Apprenticeships are a unique development method, which involves learning knowledge and then applying this in a real workplace,' Ilona says. 'Embedding training in this way can be really effective for apprentices in helping increase their capabilities and strengthening their skill set.'

As she points out, graduates have the knowledge but not necessarily the practical experience to support the translation of that knowledge into the workplace. 'Graduates' skills tend to be more theoretical in nature, so the benefit for us of someone completing an apprenticeship is that it helps connect the dots and apply learnt theory into the workplace.'

Ilona also notes that apprenticeships are challenging: 'You need to be self-motivated and able to balance work, study and personal life demands, so they aren't necessarily right for everyone. However, if someone is keen to develop and has a preference for practical learning methods, then an apprenticeship could be a great option to consider.'

Additional advice that Ilona would give to any apprentice is:

● don't be afraid to ask for help if you need it; whether that's time off from the job to focus on your development or studies, or if you need help to understand something that just isn't going in

● remember the support network around you, so make sure you speak to your coach, your mentor, your manager or even a colleague

● be prepared to complete study in your own time – the majority of learning will take place at work, but inevitably you'll need to be willing to put in some hours of your own time if you are keen to succeed

● be curious – have an open mind and be inquisitive about what's going on around you.

And for businesses considering providing apprenticeships, Ilona encourages them to do so and to embrace the process by working this offering into their People strategy. 'There are huge benefits that apprentices can bring, including helping to minimise challenges all businesses are facing, such as retention.'

# Section 7
# Getting a great
# apprenticeship

# Introduction to Section 7: Getting a great apprenticeship

You understand the options available to you. You understand yourself. You have identified apprenticeships that look right for you and begun to evaluate them.

You are ready to apply…

Simply knowing that you want an apprenticeship is not enough – you now need to convince an employer that you are worth their time and their money. You will also need to convince the employer's chosen training provider that you are going to be a good learner.

But how do you do this if you haven't had a job before? Surely the whole point of an apprenticeship is that it gives a chance to someone who is just starting out, who by definition does not have experience?

Well, this is true – and this is often why employers create apprenticeship opportunities aimed at people starting out in their careers. But they need more than your promises: saying 'I'm passionate' about something is not enough – you need to *do* more.

You need to be able to *show* them, somehow, that this is something you really want to do. As Louis Warner, Chief Operating Officer of Founders Factory, an ex-apprentice and a frequent employer of apprentices says, 'You need to be able to give the employer a number of different signals that you are right for the role.'

The 'signals' that Louis is talking about include the following sorts of things.

- You have done things in your spare time that show the employer that this is something you are serious about and could commit to.
- You have had a relevant part-time job or a side-hustle that shows that this is something you take seriously.

- You have done lots of research, so even if you don't have direct practical experience, you know your stuff enough to show an employer that you are ready and willing to take the inevitable ups and downs of a job in your chosen area.

- Maybe you have a family member who has experience in the same field and you have spoken to them a lot about their work – this gives you credibility when you talk about working in the same field.

Remember, don't *tell* the employer that this is your dream opportunity; *show* them that it is.

Here is what you need to do to maximise your chances of success when applying for apprenticeships.

- Know your story.
- Navigate the application process effectively.
- Assess the apprenticeship.
- Assess the employer.
- Respond appropriately to the outcome.

# 7.1 Know your 'story' for each apprenticeship

Think about each apprenticeship that you are applying for as though it was the *only* one you were applying for. Now think about the 'story' of why you are applying for it. Make full use of all the research and thinking you've done.

If you have a clear story in your head for each application, you will be clear on why you are applying for it. As a result, your application will be better and take less time: you will avoid those agonising minutes of staring at the empty screen wondering how to begin. Developing your story for each application is definitely worth an hour of your time (and the more you do for different apprenticeships, the better you will get and the easier it will become).

For each apprenticeship imagine you are being asked five questions by the employer.

1.  'Why do you want to do an apprenticeship?'
2.  'Why do you want to work in this occupation/sector?'
3.  'Why do you want to work for our organisation?'
4.  'Why do you want this role in particular?'
5.  'Why should we hire you in particular for this role?'

Then re-read the job advert. Research the company to see if you can find out even more.

Once you have a clear idea of what they are looking for, come up with initial answers for each of the five questions. Are you convinced with these answers? Test them out on a friend or family member. Are they convinced? Where there are gaps in your answers, see if you can fill them – it may be quicker than you think to find someone to talk to, undertake a bit of research or have a go at doing something yourself, like getting a day's work experience or shadowing in a similar employer.

## 1. 'Why do you want to do an apprenticeship?'

Things to consider.

- Your desire to 'get going' with your career.
- Your beliefs about the value of choosing an apprenticeship over going to university.
- Your understanding of how employers are changing their perceptions about apprenticeships.
- The value to you of the apprenticeship qualification.

You should be able to complete this sentence in a way that convinces you:

*'I want to go down the apprenticeship route because…'*

## 2. 'Why do you want to work in this occupation/sector?'

The second part of your 'story' is about the occupation and sector. Drawing heavily on the research you have done in Sections 5 and 6, explain why you are interested in an apprenticeship in the occupation and/or sector you are applying for. Think about why this is exciting for you, and why you think you have the strengths and attributes that are right for it.

Employers may worry that people who have never worked in that occupation or sector before will have an 'idealised' view of it and will 'drop out' once they see what it is really like. So one of your jobs in the application process is to show them that you have a realistic understanding of the role – both the good and the bad.

Think through what might be hard about this occupation and why you believe you will cope with the challenges well. Indeed, if you think that the challenges are something you will relish then that's definitely something to focus on. For example, if you are applying for an apprenticeship that involves outdoor work and you love working outdoors (even on a cold November day!), then let them know this as it will reassure and even excite the person looking at your application.

You should be able to complete this sentence in a way that convinces you:

*'I want to be in this [name of this occupation and/or sector] because…'*

### 3. 'Why do you want to work for our organisation?'

Next is the all-important task of thinking through why you want to work for *them* in particular. This is important. They want to hear that you will be enthusiastic, and that your expectations about working for them are accurate. They need to check that you will be happy and that their colleagues will enjoy having you around.

In addition, they are only human and will feel happy and reassured about *their* continued choice to work for that organisation if you articulate convincingly why you think they would be great to work for – a great way to make a subtle but important connection with them!

Make sure that your research on the employer (see previous section) is fresh in your mind so that you can come up with a really good second half of this sentence:
*'I want to work for you because...'*

### 4. 'Why do you want this role in particular?'

Be clear on why the particular role you are applying for is right for you. Think about what aspects of the job description particularly appeal to you and why you think you would be good at them (link back to what you enjoy doing and your strengths). Think about why it would be a good place for you to learn, and why that learning would excite and motivate you.

You should be able to complete this sentence in a way that convinces you:
*'I want this particular role in your organisation because...'*

### 5. 'Why will you be a good person for us to hire?'

Keep in mind what you enjoy and your strengths. Think about what the employer wants from the person they are hiring. Think about how your experience – whether in your home life, at school, through work experience or through volunteering – can show that you have skills, knowledge or approaches to life and work that match what they are looking for. Remember: it is never too late to go and get some work or volunteering experience – even if only for a day or two – to create examples that you can talk about.

You should be able to complete this sentence in a way that convinces you:

*'I will be a good person for you to hire into this role because...'*

Use the following **Develop your story Tool (also available to download at indigo.careers/understanding_apprenticeships)** as a template for mapping out your story for each apprenticeship:

## *Develop your story*

| | Apprenticeship 1 | Apprenticeship 2 | Apprenticeship 3 |
|---|---|---|---|
| *'I want to go down the apprenticeship route because...'* | | | |
| *'I want to be a [insert the name of someone doing this occupation] because...'* | | | |
| *'I want to work for [the employer] because...'* | | | |
| *'I want this particular role in your organisation because...'* | | | |
| *'I will be a good person for you to hire into this role because...'* | | | |

Now that you have thought through your story, you are ready to begin the application process.

# 7.2 Navigating the application process

Every application process will be slightly different, but is likely to follow a sequence of four stages.

1. Some sort of initial application where you have to tell the employer about yourself and, normally, something about why you want this apprenticeship.

2. A telephone call to make sure your application is legitimate and sincere, which might also be a 'first round' interview where they will ask you more questions about yourself and why you want the apprenticeship.

3. An interview of some sort.

4. An assessment centre of some sort.

Find out what the exact process is for each apprenticeship you are applying for. This means you can prepare effectively – if you know what's coming and what's expected, you will do better – and can show to the employer that you have an eye for detail. In other words just making this enquiry is an easy way to impress them.

Lots of employers, especially those that are not huge companies, will rely heavily on their apprenticeship training provider to help them with the recruitment process, particularly at the first stages (application, telephone interviews, etc.). Be aware of this, both so that you understand what is going on, and also because you may want to emphasise slightly different things to the training provider and slightly different things to the employer: for a training provider, your commitment to the apprenticeship qualification will be especially important for them (they get left out of pocket if you don't complete the apprenticeship); for the employer it will be more to do with your willingness to learn how to do the job.

Here are the five things that you need to make sure you show the employer and training provider at all stages of the application process:

i. You have a coherent, interesting and convincing 'story' about you and why you want this apprenticeship (see Chapter 7.1).

ii. You are enthusiastic about doing the job *and* about the opportunity to get an apprenticeship qualification at the same time.

iii. You are ambitious – you want to do well, both in your job and in the apprenticeship.

iv. You are diligent: punctual, appropriately dressed, you have completed any pre-assessments they have asked of you, you have visibly put effort in and prepared for this process – all this shows them that you are reliable.

v. You are likeable: you are polite, you smile, you are humble and clearly eager to learn and prove yourself, but you are not shy about your ambitions for yourself.

Here are some pointers on the different stages:

# 1. Initial application process

- Follow their instructions: if they want a CV and a covering letter, do a CV and a covering letter; if they want you to write 500 words on something, write 500 words on it (not 200 and not 700).

- Don't worry about writing beautifully, but do use the spellchecker and get someone else to read what you have written (especially if it is an online form) to spot typos.

- Write a first draft and come back to it a day later – you will spot a myriad of opportunities to make it better.

- Be honest – there is no point exaggerating or saying something that isn't true. If you do get through to subsequent stages and they find out that something you have said is not true then it is both embarrassing and a waste of everyone's time (including yours).

- But make sure you 'sell' your story to them; this is different from exaggerating and certainly different from being dishonest. Instead, think about what will be important to the person looking at your application; use positive words wherever you can; use facts and numbers to show that what you are saying is true; try to avoid relying on words like 'really' or 'very' – they often serve to reveal that you are overstating a claim rather than anything else!

- Facts and figures are always better than an unsubstantiated claim. For example, 'I have volunteered every Saturday morning for the last nine months at the local Cancer Research shop' is stronger than 'I have been a really committed volunteer for a long time for a local charity.'

- Leave plenty of time – there is nothing more annoying or upsetting than missing out on a dream opportunity because your WiFi packs in just as you are about to hit 'send'.

### A note on your CV

Lots of job applications (but not all) will expect some sort of CV. Schools, colleges and careers advisors will be able to help you with your CV. As it is highly personal, I am not going to spend much time on it other than to share five key tips for making your CV as effective as possible.

   **i.**   Stick to the usual conventions (people reading lots of CVs typically don't like surprises where they have to think hard to figure out the format of a 'wacky' or 'creative' CV).

   **ii.**   Tailor your CV for every application, putting the things that are more important upfront.

  **iii.**   Get someone else to check each and every one – it's amazing how little typos can sneak in or how something that you think makes good sense in fact does not.

  **iv.**   Explain how your key experiences or attributes are relevant to this application.

   **v.**   Include a short paragraph (whether at the top or bottom) that tells your 'story' in short, including your ambitions and what you are looking to achieve from this role.

Apply these five tips to any covering letter as well. Show them that you have done your research on the occupation, the sector, them as a business and the role.

## 2. First telephone call

Often, but not always, the first response to your application will be some sort of telephone call. This could well be from the employer's training provider, someone in the employer's recruitment team or one of your prospective future colleagues.

If they have fixed a time with you in advance, be ready at least five minutes before they call so that your heart rate is down, your voice is normal, and you are not flustered. If they ring out of the blue and it is not a good time, say so – politely – and see if you can rearrange a better time.

Remember, this is the first time they will have heard your voice, so the impression you make is key. Answer the questions as best you can, taking your time and asking them to clarify any questions if you are unsure what they are asking. If you have done your research properly and have prepared your 'story' about why you want this apprenticeship and why you are right for it, then this call should be nothing to fear! You will just need to be yourself.

If they liked your application, and your first telephone call has confirmed that you are a good candidate, then you are likely to be invited through to the next stage, which will be some sort of interview, or assessment, or both. Let's have a look at each in turn…

## 3. Interview

This is the one part that typically makes candidates nervous. But it doesn't have to, if you have done your preparation. Remember if you come into any interview with a clear understanding of yourself, a clear understanding and story about why you want this apprenticeship with this employer and what you can bring to it, you will have nothing to worry about what they might ask or how you will answer.

Here are some extra tips, just to help keep the nerves at bay.

- *Be yourself.* If they decide to hire you and you end up working with them for eight hours a day, five days a week, then you will have to be yourself – so you might as well start at the interview. If you don't get the job, and you have been yourself, then that apprenticeship probably was not right for you; learn the lessons you can and you will be even better for your next application.

- *Be early.* If there's a bus that will get you there 5 minutes beforehand, get the earlier one that gets you there 20 minutes early; you can't blame the bus if you're late. Show them you are reliable by arriving somewhere between 20 and 15 minutes early. That will also give you a chance to catch your breath, get used to the surroundings and not be flustered going into the interview room.

- *Dress appropriately*. Ring them beforehand and ask what the dress code is for your interview. If, for some reason, you cannot get through to anyone, have a look at their company website and see if you can get hints on what is appropriate. If in doubt, err on the side of being too smart rather than too casual.

- *Smile!* Even if it's a nervous smile, this will communicate to the employer that you are a nice person to have around. Remember, human beings are hard wired to respond positively to a smile.

- *Take your time with your answers*. If you don't understand a question, ask them if they can explain or rephrase it. This will do three things: one, it will help you understand the question better and improve your chances of giving a good answer; two, it will buy you some time to get your thoughts together; and three, it will look good – someone who checks their interview questions is likely to be the kind of person who checks when they are given a task: be that person!

- *Check your answers with them*. If you think an answer you have given is not very good, then just check by asking the interviewer something like, 'Is that the kind of answer you were looking for?'. The interviewer will almost certainly give you another chance if they were not convinced by your first answer, and will like you because you have removed the potential awkwardness from the situation. I do not mean that you do this after every question, but if a question is a bit tricky or the person interviewing you looks a bit puzzled or concerned, checking in shows that you have awareness and thoughtfulness.

- *Have your questions for them ready*. If you have done your research as you should have done, then you will probably have some questions in mind. The kind of questions that work well are ones about what the role is actually like, what attributes the person they are hiring should have and about how they will be able to support you to succeed in your apprenticeship. It's also totally okay to ask about the next stage of the application process, but try to make sure this is not your only question. Remember, if you *don't* ask any questions, then you risk coming across as lacking interest in them and in the role, neither of which is a good thing.

Something that can make a *big* difference is to make sure you speak to whoever has interviewed you after the interview, whether or not you were successful in getting through to the next round. Ask them what they liked about you and what they did not. If you have got through to the next stage, then you will know what to focus on and what to improve. And if you were unsuccessful, you will come away with some brilliant lessons and insights that you can apply to make your next application even better.

## 4. Assessment centre

Often the interview will be the final process and you will either get the job offer then or get the bad news that you have not been successful this time.

However, some employers, particularly bigger ones, will want to assess you further, alongside other candidates. This is often called the 'assessment centre', but they may call it something else.

The assessment centre can often be fun. But it can also be a bit intimidating, not least when you meet your fellow candidates who you are competing with for the role(s).

If the employer has given you something to prepare beforehand, then make sure you do that. Nothing conveys that you are not really that interested in a job opportunity more than *not* doing something that they have asked you to do. And, remember, some of the other candidates may not have done it, so you'll immediately be at an advantage compared to them.

Find out beforehand what the assessment centre will involve: ring the employer up and ask. Even if they don't want to tell you, they won't think any the worse of you for having asked (they will like your curiosity and organisation). And if they can give you more information, you will be better prepared on the day with less chance of any unwanted surprises.

Just remember the three golden rules for assessment centres.

    **i.**    Talk to as many people who are there as possible: fellow candidates, staff from the employer, staff from the training provider (if they are there). This will help you find out useful information, and you will relax and come across as likeable and personable – these things really matter when the people observing you come to discuss candidates at the end of the day. You don't have to be a brilliant conversationalist or have great 'small talk' – just take the opportunity to ask questions and be interested in people, and you'll quickly be up and running.

ii. Listen to the instructions for each task. In the heat of the moment, and particularly if you have done something similar before, you might easily fall into the trap of thinking you have been asked to do one thing when in fact they want you to do another.

iii. Value your fellow candidates. Lots of assessment centres have one or more team exercises and, whatever you do, do not think that putting down a teammate is ever a good thing. Yes, they are your competition for the role, but one of the main things the employer will be looking for is whether you are a team player. If you are rude to a teammate, interrupt them or do not listen to them, then the employer will get the impression that that is what you will be like to work with – not very nice. I have seen many times talented and committed individuals miss out on great roles because they have failed to heed this advice.

# 7.3 Assessing the apprenticeship

As you go through any application process, the employer will be evaluating you, assessing your strengths and weaknesses and trying to figure out whether you are the kind of person they think will succeed in the apprenticeship.

Well, you should be assessing them as well! The whole time. For an apprenticeship to work, it's not just *their* decision about you – you need to be sure that they are right for you. Remember, you are under no obligation to accept an apprenticeship should it be offered to you.

Take time to make this assessment to avoid any future regrets that you rushed into the wrong choice for you, simply because you were so excited and flattered to have been selected at the time.

The 'health warning' on this chapter, of course, is that you can never know for sure whether you've made the right decision. This is not a 'bullet-proof' process that will definitely ensure you make the best decision. But it will benefit you to take a bit of time to ask yourself the following questions:

## 1. Is the role right for you?
You will naturally get a feeling, probably quite quickly, about this. Be aware of the danger, though, that once you become excited about a particular role, you may start to see everything through that positive 'lens' and fail to spot the downsides. Remind yourself of what is important to you, and check that this opportunity is a good match for what you are looking for.

## 2. Do you like the people you have been meeting?
Humans have a well-developed instinct for who they will enjoy spending time with – it's called 'liking' someone! So if you find yourself enjoying the company of the people you are meeting then this is a good sign.

Just as you would not want to be judged solely on first impressions, try not to let first impressions be your last impressions. Keep an open mind throughout the process, as you may find that people who you were not sure of to begin with turn out to be people you do like.

If, however, over the time you spend with the organisation you are uncomfortable or uneasy, then you should trust your judgement.

Try to look beyond how upbeat and 'smiley' people are in the set pieces of recruitment, such as welcome talks. Try to talk to people away from the process, especially those not formally involved in it (e.g. the person on reception). You will get a better sense of whether people really are happy and motivated, and of what their real values are.

## 3. Is the organisation well run?

You may feel positive about the role on offer, and you may like the people you are meeting. But however great it seems, you should still ask yourself if the organisation is well run. This matters because, however lovely and positive the intentions of the people you meet, if they are unable to 'make things happen', then this could be bad news for your apprenticeship.

Previous research you have done on the employer is vital here, and you can also look out for further clues during the application process.

- Do they communicate with you clearly and in good time? Have you had to chase them to find out details of the recruitment process?
- Are their premises tidy and well organised? (I don't mean 'swanky' – but if they can't clean their toilets, then what else can't they do?)
- Do they seem stressed or calm? If they are calm, then it indicates that they know what is going on and trust that things will happen in the right way. If they are stressed, it may indicate the opposite.
- Do interviews and assessment exercises happen smoothly? Are they able to explain them well? If not, it may indicate that they have not properly prepared – and if they have not properly prepared for this, there might be other things they do not properly prepare for.

## 4. Are they serious about skills development?

It is important for you that the employer is prepared to invest time, money and energy developing new people like you, even if it may take many months for you to 'pay back' that investment.

You will naturally get an impression of how the organisation thinks about skills and people development, but you should definitely ask them about it specifically, and in a way that gets 'under the skin' of the issue. So, rather than asking 'Are you committed to developing the skills of your staff?' – I mean, who would say 'no' to that?! – ask something a bit more searching, such as 'How do you show your staff in practical terms how you are committed to developing their skills?'.

Remember, they may have other reasons for running an apprenticeship programme, so it is important to test their motives. For example, perhaps they think it will make them look good to customers or investors, or cynically want to only pay the apprenticeship minimum wage, or just want to spend their apprenticeship levy, or maybe they like the idea of Government grants.

## 5. Are they serious about apprenticeships specifically?

What matters to you is that they are committed to making apprenticeships work. This means that they understand and believe in some of the key things that make an apprenticeship special: the fact that it runs for at least a year, the fact that your line manager is crucial to the process, the blend of on-the-job and off-the-job learning (and recognising that both are equally important), and an appreciation of the need for the rules and regulations that surround an apprenticeship.

To find out quite quickly what their views on apprenticeships are, a good question to ask them is what do they see as the strengths and weaknesses of the apprenticeship approach. You are not looking for how 'polished' their answers are but for how committed they are.

So, if you do get an offer of an apprenticeship, take 20 minutes to write down your thoughts on each of the five questions above, and discuss them with someone whose opinion you trust. This will help you to decide whether this is the right apprenticeship for you.

# 7.4 Responding appropriately

At some point you will find out if your application has been successful or not. Whether it is the news you wanted or it's a 'no', you need to respond. Here's how to do this well:

If you've been successful, here's what to do.

- Be enthusiastic! They will have spent a lot of time and effort on getting you this far, and they will want to know that you care at least as much as they do.
- Say thank you for their decision and for the process.
- If you are not sure it's right for you, or if you are in that lovely but difficult position of having more than one offer to consider, ask if you can have some time to consider their offer, perhaps mentioning that you want to talk to family or friends. While they may be disappointed that they don't get an initial 'yes', they will be impressed that you are taking your time and being considerate.
- Fix the next steps with your new employer: your starting date, when you will get a contract to sign, sending them your bank details (so you can get paid!), or fixing a date when you might go to meet your colleagues before you start. Make sure you understand what happens next – and write it all down!

If you have been unsuccessful, here's what to do.

- Be gracious. If they haven't offered you the role, it will be for a good reason (in 99.99% of cases!), so accept their view.
- Be thankful for the opportunity of going through the process; let them know how much you enjoyed it and what you learned.
- Find out what they thought about you – not just what you can improve, but ask them what they liked about you and where they saw your strengths. This means you will gain insight and also retain some confidence for your next application.
- Ask them if they would like you to apply again if they are recruiting in the future; this sends a great message about your enthusiasm and, you never know, if the person they do offer it to drops out, maybe they will come back to you!

# Section 7 summary: Getting a great apprenticeship

To get the apprenticeship you want, you need to do more than say you want it – you need to provide the potential employer with the signals that you are ready for it.

You first need to know what your 'story' is for each and every apprenticeship you apply for: why you want an apprenticeship; why you want to join this particular occupation; why you want to work for that organisation; why you want that role in particular; and why you will be a great hire for them to make.

This will then stand you in great stead as you go through the likely stages of the application.

- The initial application itself: stick to what the employer has asked for and is expecting, keep it factual and honest – but make sure you 'sell' yourself in your CV, covering letter and any other written material they ask for.

- The first telephone call (or other first contact): take this as seriously as any other part of the process, it is your first chance to make a great impression.

- The interview: be prepared (check in with the employer on the interview process and do further research on them as an organisation), smile, take your time with your answers and don't be afraid to check the meaning of a question; have some questions ready for them at the end.

- Assessment centre (or equivalent): check beforehand what is expected from you; when you are there, talk to as many people as you can (to find out more, to relax and to show your positive personality); listen carefully to the instructions; and, finally, treat your fellow candidates with respect.

- Don't forget that it is not just them assessing you – you are also assessing them. You are under no obligation to accept an apprenticeship should it be offered to you. Ask yourself key questions about the role and the organisation.

- Whatever the outcome of the process, respond appropriately – and always with grace.

### APPRENTICE CASE STUDY: JACK BONFIELD

Patience, teamwork and an eye for aesthetic detail – the key attributes of Jack Bonfield's apprenticeship story.

Jack, by his own admission, was not successful at school. He left before the end of year 11, and – through friends and family contacts – began to work on various building sites. His search for an apprenticeship began then, but without luck. 'Times were different then – there wasn't the same support for apprenticeships that there is now. I found I had a knack for the work, but I had to be really patient.' It would take eight years before he finally began his apprenticeship in a technical branch of roofing (waterproof membrane installation), with the firm he now works for as a full-time employee.

'It has been totally worth the wait, and I'm really glad I never gave up on finding an apprenticeship – even though at times I thought it would never happen.'

He gives huge credit to the apprenticeship for how it has enabled him to create a strong foundation for the rest of his career. Jack has an interesting insight here: the qualification, and the theoretical side of his studies, meant that he could engage in conversations with more senior people and other tradespeople when on site, because he understood what they were talking about. Once it was clear to them that he had valuable knowledge to input, he found more opportunities coming his way, which gave him the confidence to take on a leadership role. This in turn has accelerated his knowledge acquisition, and so he finds himself in a virtuous circle in which knowledge leads to opportunities, which lead to more knowledge, more opportunities and so on – all kick-started by the apprenticeship.

'My character has really been built through this apprenticeship, and I've managed to create a really good network, including with others doing the same apprenticeship as me – it's great to know that you are sharing that journey with others like you. And these people will be great connections in the future, whether I'm in a site supervisor role or even when I'm setting up my own firm.'

Jack takes obvious pride in the quality of the work he does, undertaking the technically demanding work of creating waterproof building solutions. Not only does it require significant technical skills where precision is essential, there is an aesthetic aspect to it. 'I really enjoy the design process: how to use colours, how to mix different materials for different effects and purposes; and I like it when we have completed an installation and you can see how it's really working in practice.' Jack mentions as well how much he enjoys the camaraderie of being on site with other colleagues, often in all sorts of weather.

His advice to young people like him: 'Get started. Everything can seem really far away while you are still and haven't got moving yet; but as soon as you are moving, you start to open doors that lead to more doors and so on. And don't underestimate the importance of a formal qualification, like an apprenticeship. I haven't yet completed my apprenticeship and already my company are talking about me taking on higher roles – and I see other roofers who are way older than me who haven't progressed because they don't have the formal qualification that I'm getting.'

## EMPLOYER CASE STUDY: NETWORK RAIL

Network Rail is the organisation responsible for maintaining all of the railways in the UK, employing over 23,000 people throughout the country. It looks after some of the biggest train stations as well, such as Leeds and Bristol Temple Meads. Network Rail is at the heart of our national infrastructure.

The rail industry faces a continuous skills crunch – there just aren't enough people with the necessary skills available to hire. So Network Rail has to find and train people themselves. It does this primarily through apprenticeships, currently employing 1,600 apprentices on different programmes in locations across the country.

Over 800 people are doing the Level 3 Rail Engineering programme, focused on railway maintenance: signalling, the track itself, overhead lines, power distribution and telecommunications. Another 300 are on engineering apprenticeships between Levels 4 and 7; a further 300 or so have been recruited locally to various roles; and there are nearly 150 apprentices in leadership and project management. Network Rail also recruits around 150 graduates a year.

'Apprenticeships work really well for us,' says Hannah Connors, Head of Apprenticeship Delivery. 'We can take a young person and get them pretty quickly to a high level of operational productivity. The structure and linear nature of a higher level apprenticeship means the apprentice is moving fast.'

Apprenticeships work for the people doing them too: 'Our apprentices benefit from a rapid learning cycle: they can implement what they are learning, they can see its relevance. The money helps too – although starting salaries are not high, many progress quickly. There are a number of people who qualified as apprentices getting on the housing ladder sooner than their peers who go down other routes.'

She also notes other advantages to doing an apprenticeship, including an interesting one around communication: 'Apprentices learn quickly that communication is about adapting to the "room", the people you are with at a given moment, not about being "eloquent". Apprentices often gain the required emotional intelligence for this quicker than graduates, who may have had three years honing skills but away from real-life situations.'

Her advice to anyone doing an apprenticeship is clear: 'Make the most of the opportunities, find out what all the support mechanisms are, and do not be shy about asking for support and clarity whenever you need it.'

# Section 8
# Apprenticeships are for everyone

# Introduction to section 8: Apprenticeships are for everyone

Apprenticeships are for everyone.

But getting an apprenticeship that is right for you is not easy. And some people may face additional challenges in securing that apprenticeship.

This section takes a quick look at what it means for people in certain groups who may face additional hurdles and how they can best approach the apprenticeship 'market'.

There is a chapter for you if you:

- are from a minority ethnic community
- have a learning difficulty/disability, a physical disability, or experience mental health and/or emotional challenges
- are care-experienced
- are not in employment, education or training (NEET).

Whether you are in one or more of these groups, or whether you are just concerned about apprenticeships and the application process, make sure you make use of some excellent organisations who are dedicated to supporting people just like you. This includes the Association of Apprentices (associationofapprentices.org.uk), a growing network of supportive apprentices which has valuable resources to help you address a whole range of issues, and Amazing Apprenticeships (amazingapprenticeships.com).

# 8.1 People from a minority ethnic background

People from a minority ethnic background can face additional barriers when it comes to getting an apprenticeship. For example, the population of the UK from a black, Asian and minority ethnic background is 18%, but the percentage of apprentices who are from such a background is just 14%.

While there is no clear evidence for why this is the case, there appear to be two kinds of barriers.

The first is part of the bigger picture of employment challenges that people with minority ethnic backgrounds face. For example, a 2018 study by Oxford University found that black, Asian and minority ethnic applicants had to apply for 60% more roles than a white person of British origin to secure a job. Even where this is not overt racism, there is still a chance that some people are unconsciously more likely to hire people from a similar background to themselves than someone from another background.

If you are in a situation like this, remember that there are many employers who really don't care about your background – they are just looking to find the best person for the job. And there are others who are actively looking to diversify their workforce in order to have better insight and resilience. Do your research to find out whether an employer is looking to diversify, at which point your background can become your asset.

There is also some evidence to suggest that people from a minority ethnic background are more likely to drop out of their apprenticeship than other groups. The evidence for why this happens is still not yet well developed, but it may be to do with how included an apprentice feels. For example, one person I spoke to noted that if going for a drink after work is seen as a key place where employees bond, that may not be a comfortable environment for someone who is Muslim and a non-drinker. Clearly while the onus should be on employers to make sure everyone is included, you can nonetheless find out if an employer will be inclusive and even ask them to be so. Talk to others in a similar position and find out how they handle this, and lean on organisations like the Association of Apprentices to help.

The second kind of barrier is rather different. For many minority ethnic communities, especially where existing relatives have made significant sacrifices to raise their family in the UK, going to university carries extra significance: it can signal to them and their community that they have reached a threshold of acceptance in the UK. For one of their children – especially one who is seen as academically bright – to turn down the possibility of going to university seems to be a rejection of this aspiration too.

This is a tough one to counter. Start talking to your parents and loved ones early, encourage them to find out about apprenticeships themselves, and share with them the reasons why university might not be right for you. You may have to be patient and kind to them, but do not forget to make sure your future is your number one priority – if you end up being happy and successful, they will soon forget that you didn't go to university. If you want advice, reach out to the Multicultural Apprenticeship Alliance to see what insight and support you can get.

# 8.2 People with special educational needs, disabilities and other additional needs

You may have a disability (physical or mental), be neurodivergent or experience a condition that makes accessing work harder (e.g. anxiety). Apprenticeships can work for you as well.

Employers are required by law to make reasonable adjustments for people who have disabilities and conditions. These might be adjustments to the physical workspace, or it could be to enable a different work routine or pattern.

The Government's Access to Work scheme (gov.uk/access-to-work or able-futures.co.uk) exists to support people with practical support. The combination of your employer making reasonable adjustments together with the help from Access to Work could make a real difference for you. Have a look and encourage any potential employer to look at this too: don't assume they already know about it.

Look for companies who have the 'Disability Confident employer' badge – this should be displayed on their website and on job application documents. By being part of this scheme, it shows they have made a specific commitment to employing people who have disabilities.

You may wonder when (or even whether) you should declare your disability. Your fear may be that by declaring it too early, you will be ruled out (even if the discrimination is unconscious) before you have even had a chance. You may hope that, once the employer gets to know you and likes you, when you inform them you have a disability it will no longer be an issue.

The downside of this approach is, of course, that you might appear dishonest – and that, even though they have grown to like you, they cannot ignore the fact that you have not declared something that you could have.

A good reason to tell them early on in the application process is that they are then bound by the Equality Act 2010 (i.e, by law) to treat you fairly and to make reasonable adjustments. However, if you have not told them, then the legislation does not apply.

You need to make your own call on this, and it is not an easy one. For advice, try talking to the Disability Rights UK helpline (free) on 0330 995 0414, search online for the Disabled Apprentice Network or look at mind.org.uk which has some useful information, e.g. around the application process: mind.org.uk/information-support/legal-rights/discrimination-at-work/telling-my-employer.

During the application process, be sure to major on the benefits to the employer of hiring you, and how having a disability or condition has given you experience, insights, skills and resilience that other candidates may not have.

Aim to build your confidence – before or alongside the process of applying for apprenticeships – with volunteering and work experience (however short to begin with). This will really support your self-belief and your ability to secure the apprenticeship you want.

Here's a bit more on some specific circumstances that may be relevant to you.

## 1. If you are neurodivergent

Neurodivergence includes things like autism, ADHD, dyslexia, dysgraphia and dyscalculia, as well as Tourette's syndrome. Neurodivergent people may have one or more of these types of neurodivergence.

It remains challenging for neurodivergent people to secure jobs, mainly because neurotypical people are uncertain how to respond to their neurodivergence, and often fail to see the potential of the person, focusing instead on the 'difference'. The Office for National Statistics (2021) reported that only 22% of autistic adults are in any kind of employment.

However, things are beginning to improve. Organisations like Neurodiversity in Business (neurodiversityinbusiness.org) are generating considerable support from a growing number of big employers, helping them to see the valuable contribution that neurodivergent people can make. Companies such as Bupa, EY, Google, Salesforce, IBM and Microsoft are all proactively engaged in initiatives to hire neurodivergent people.

Here is the advice from Neurodiversity In Business if you are neurodivergent.

- Make your own decisions – you know yourself best.
- Others should not make assumptions about what you can and cannot do.
- Focus on what you are good at, not on what you struggle with.
- Remind people that what may seem a 'safe' or 'easy' career to them may not seem that way to you (and vice versa).

Work with your training provider to ensure they can adapt the learning environment to suit your needs. It is also sensible to talk to them and the employer about the environment in which you will be expected to work and learn, to see if there are any adjustments they can make that will help. If transport and logistics is a particular issue for you, then make sure you do your research on this for any potential apprenticeship.

It may also be sensible to point your employer to the advice that national organisations like Neurodiversity in Business can provide. There may be local organisations that do the same thing, for example Digital Advantage in Manchester. These organisations can support employers to get the best out of neurodivergent employees, such as providing detailed guidance on workplace protocols and providing 'buddy' or mentor schemes.

## 2. If you have a physical disability or condition

Around 18% of the UK population have a disability of some sort, but only just over 12% of people starting apprenticeships do.

Changes triggered by the pandemic in working patterns have been beneficial in this regard, e.g. acceptance of working from home for at least some of the time. Employers are required to make 'reasonable adjustments', but what 'reasonable' means will, of course, vary depending on the situation.

Nonetheless, it is likely that some occupations will be hard for an employer to make reasonable adjustments for. But it is also true that many employers now have experience of hiring people with disabilities, and there is growing understanding and acceptance that people with disabilities have just as much to offer as anyone else, and sometimes more so because of their particular insights and empathy.

There may also, sadly, be discrimination, if people who are making the hiring decisions – mistakenly – think that employing someone with a physical disability is riskier than employing someone who does not.

Make sure you research potential employers, in particular looking out for whether they have Diversity, Equality and Inclusion (DEI) policies and/or are otherwise positive towards people with disabilities. You may find that larger employers are more likely to be in this category than smaller ones – but always find out. If it is not apparent from their website, then give them a call. By contacting them, not only will you find out the 'official' answer, you will also get a feel for how real their commitment is and – the icing on the cake of this approach – you will make an impression on them, such that if you do choose to apply, your application may well stick out positively.

## 3. If you have learning difficulties

If you had a Special Educational Needs diagnosis while at school, that does not mean that you cannot do an apprenticeship. Focus on what you enjoy and what you can do.

There is flexibility in how apprenticeships can be delivered that may make it possible for you to complete one. For example, you may get an exemption so that you do not have to achieve the specified levels in English and maths. It is also possible to do an apprenticeship part time.

Crucially, there is also financial support available for your employer (£1,000 plus full payment of the apprenticeship training fees) and your training provider (up to £19,000) to provide the additional support you may need.

There are also 'supported internships' available for people who are 16–24 with an Education, Health and Care Plan (EHCP). Lasting up to six months, a supported internship combines a study programme (via classroom learning) with real experience in a supported job placement.

Although they are unpaid, they can be a great way to test the water with a particular employer or occupation, and can lead directly to employment or, if you decide to apply for another apprenticeship afterwards, they give you fantastic hands-on work experience to talk about.

## 4. If you have mental or emotional health challenges

There are an increasing number of people who are succeeding in the workplace while experiencing mental health challenges. These positive role models include apprentices. However, many of the same issues that people with physical disabilities face are also faced by those with mental health challenges in terms of bias, whether conscious or unconscious. While the stigma associated with mental health challenges is decreasing, it can still be an issue.

However, there are some things to consider.

- Apprenticeships, if delivered well, provide quite a lot of natural structure, with lots of people around you to support you; ask questions to help you gauge the level of structure and support available from both your employer and training provider.

- Research which apprenticeships are going to best fit with your needs; for example, if anxiety is an issue, aim for apprenticeships where the work and study is likely to be more structured and predictable.

- Remember that employers have a legal duty of care towards you as an employee, in terms of making sure things are safe for you, that you are not discriminated against, and they need to carry out risk assessments – do not be afraid to ask employers about how they fulfil this duty of care for people like you.

# 8.3 People who are care-experienced

People who have been in care are likely to come to the apprenticeships market with extra challenges. In practical terms, it often means that there are few family members and friends-of-family networks through which you can find out about different careers and through which to get different work-related opportunities, from work experience to actual apprenticeships and jobs. It is also harder to get support and encouragement as you go through applications.

The good news is, the Government recognises these challenges and has put in place meaningful financial incentives for you and for employers and training providers who give you the opportunity. You can get a bursary of £3,000, on top of your salary, if you get an apprenticeship; while employers and training providers get a cash sum if they provide you with an apprenticeship.

My advice is to research employers who have an explicit and strong DEI policy (Diversity, Equality and Inclusion), and contact them beforehand to both find out what they do to help people like you *and* to boost the chances of them remembering you if you do apply.

Also research and contact training providers and colleges who deliver apprenticeships in the areas and occupations you are interested in. They may have a particular focus on care leavers; if they don't, you can tell them about the grants they can get for helping you out (and in the process you will make a very positive impression on them).

# 8.4 People who are not in employment, education or training (NEET)

If you are in a position where you are not in employment, education or training (NEET in government jargon) you are certainly not alone – according to the Office for National Statistics, 788,000 16–24-year-olds were in this position in October to December 2022.

There are many reasons why you might be in this position, many of which may be because of circumstances beyond your control. However, some employers might wrongly interpret you being 'NEET' as showing that you do not care about your career or that there is something preventing you from getting started. This might be completely unfair! But you need to be prepared to face this potential challenge head on.

The good news? It *is* possible to change their minds! And, indeed, many employers are keen to spot a talented young person who just needs a break – you need to show them that person is you.

It will help a lot to get some purposeful activity under your belt. This does not have to be paid work, it could be as a volunteer. Do not be shy about asking organisations whether they can use your time, skills and enthusiasm and give you that vital opportunity at the same time.

There are also now a growing number of government-funded 'bootcamps' that are free and aimed exactly at people in your situation. These involve a mixture of some off-the-job learning and some work experience activity with a real employer. While the learning and support from the training provider is going to be useful, the most valuable part of this is the contact with any employers. Have as many conversations as you can with everyone you come across at the employers who are involved – ask lots of questions, find out what upcoming jobs and apprenticeships there are, and put yourself forward for as many tasks as you can.

There are many charities, both national (such as The Prince's Trust) and local whose purpose is to help those in your circumstances find ways into good careers – search them out and don't be afraid to contact them.

It can be really hard to be in this position when all you want is to show what you can do. Remember that getting your career started is often the hardest part – what you may well need is your first entry into paid employment and the rest will follow. It may be that you cannot get your dream apprenticeship to begin with, or even any apprenticeship – you may have to start with less formal jobs to get yourself going, with an apprenticeship coming later.

But, as for everyone who faces additional challenges in securing an apprenticeship, your determination will shine through and will, I believe, get you where you want to go in the end.

# Section 8 summary: Apprenticeships are for everyone

You may face additional challenges when considering and applying for apprenticeships.

The good news, regardless of what particular issues you face, is that:

- Things are changing for the better (albeit quite slowly), with big firms in particular prioritising recruitment of people from diverse backgrounds and circumstances.

- There are practical steps and sources of support out there from people and organisations who really want to help you.

- The law is on your side and there are tangible measures in place to help employers give you the opportunity you want.

## APPRENTICE CASE STUDY: GEORGE EILOART

George never had any intention of going to university: from a very young age, he remembers he just wanted to do rather than learn. In part, this was because of his severe dyslexia, which meant that there simply was not that much enjoyment or payback from academic studies; and, in part, because he knew he enjoyed setting up little businesses and doing things outside of studies.

After GCSEs he first floated the idea of an apprenticeship to his parents – they were not keen, mainly because at the time it was not seen as an aspirational route. He started a BTEC at college in a vocational subject, but it was not what he wanted. One of his peers applied for an apprenticeship and he discovered that, in fact, there were all sorts of apprenticeships available.

He applied for an apprenticeship at Facebook. He was unsuccessful – but he had showed his parents two things: first, that major companies were now taking apprenticeships seriously, and secondly, that when the goal was right, he could be seriously motivated and organised.

George was not disheartened by missing out on his dream apprenticeship, and on reflection is very positive: 'I am genuinely glad I didn't get the Facebook apprenticeship. The career I have had since, based on the apprenticeship that I *did* get has been amazing. It just goes to show that the most glamorous and "sexy" job is not necessarily the best one for you as an individual.'

The career he has had so far has seen him take on a number of roles in different businesses within the venture builder Blenheim Chalcot, starting in marketing (which is what his apprenticeship was in), and moving to internal improvement, then to product development and now leading business development for the EMEA region (Europe, Middle East and Africa) for technology startup EnglishScore.

'I learned quickly by watching what those around me were doing – and because I was working in different startups, I was working alongside founders and senior leaders, so I was learning from the best.' George quickly became known as a trusted pair of hands. He soon found more and more opportunities coming his way, with people trusting him to figure out what to do and make it work.

The early start to his career that his apprenticeship provided was crucial: 'It made a huge difference that I started my career so early, aged 17. An apprenticeship is a perfect way to do it: I was in the real world of work, but I had the apprenticeship structure around me which is designed to support me to develop, in a company in whose clear interests it was that I did develop.'

As he says, the expectation at the outset of an apprenticeship is that you won't be very good – but that 'as long as you are open and eager to learn and improve, you get the development and support that means you *become* good.'

George's top tip for succeeding in an apprenticeship? 'Ask lots of questions – really embrace the mantra that there is no such thing as a silly question, apart from the one you don't ask.' He says that not only do you learn incredibly quickly if you do this, you also convey strongly just how open and eager you are – attributes that your colleagues will really like. He also strongly recommends finding out about parts of the organisation beyond the part you work in.

When it comes to other advice, George points out that when he hires people he never looks at the university they went to, the degree they got or their grades – he looks at their work experience, their attitude and their drive.

He also addresses head on the concern that many people have: will I miss out on university social life if I do an apprenticeship? 'I absolutely had "uni fomo" when my friends went to uni, but in fact you can have a really good and varied social life through an apprenticeship – and when you do go to see your mates at uni, it's quite nice to be the one buying the drinks!'

For George, the financial aspect is important too; 'Not only is it the £30,000 committed to university [tuition] fees [plus living costs], it's the three years of earnings and getting a huge head start in your career that you are missing out on. All my friends – all of them – wish they had done an apprenticeship instead of going to university.

'I would love to educate parents better on the pros and cons of apprenticeships versus uni – especially as doing an apprenticeship doesn't rule you out from going to university a bit later. I also wonder whether this is a generational thing – if ever I am a parent, I can't see myself advising my teenage children to go to university without first looking at their apprenticeship options.'

### EMPLOYER CASE STUDY: IBM

IBM is one of the giants of the technology world.

Digital skills, on which a firm like IBM depends, have been in short supply for a long time. IBM, like many others, used to rely on hiring and training up university graduates and hiring people on the open recruitment market. This was not delivering the consistent pipeline of talent that they needed, so in 2010, they took the (then) pioneering step of opening up its recruitment pipeline to young people without a traditional degree via apprenticeships.

From those early experimental days, IBM has continuously grown and extended its apprenticeship programme – it now hires between 100 and 150 young people as apprentices every year, around 90% of whom are straight from school. Many start on Level 3 and Level 4 programmes, mainly in IT and junior management consultant roles, and a good proportion go on from their first apprenticeships to further apprenticeships, including degree apprenticeships. This way they use apprenticeships to build a career that rivals or even outpaces the career path of those joining the company as graduates.

As a commercially focused organisation, one of IBM's key questions at the start of this was: 'Can apprentices generate revenue for the company?'

'A resounding yes,' says Jenny Taylor, IBM's Leader of Early Professional programmes since its inception. 'Not only that, but our retention rate is 90% for the first three years of the programme and the percentage of people who complete apprenticeships and stay with us is high too – it makes it an even better recruitment route for us than university graduates.'

Jenny notes how motivated apprentices tend to be: 'To become an apprentice often requires a very deliberate and conscious choice, rather than going with the flow. That means apprentices are really dedicated and tend to put more into it. This passion, along with the knowledge, skills and behaviours they learn during the apprenticeship, are the main determinants of success.'

So committed is IBM to apprenticeships that it has now become its own training provider – a huge step, but one that means they can make the delivery of the programme match their high standards.

# Section 9
# Conclusion

Well, you have made it through to the end of this guidebook. I hope you have found it useful, and thank you for sticking with it.

I knew very little about apprenticeships when I first got involved back in 2012. I learned quickly, and saw with my own eyes the incredible power of apprenticeships – for employers and for young people alike.

I congratulate you again for considering and researching apprenticeships.

Even if you pursue another route, I hope that you have acquired a good feel for what the apprenticeship option is, and perhaps have picked up some hints and tips that will help you, even as you pursue a different route. If it has helped you rule out apprenticeships as an option for you, then I am glad as well – my goal has been to help people make the right decision for them.

For those of you who are going down the apprenticeship route, I think that is an excellent choice. The opportunities to get a 'fast start' to your career are fantastic, and to start to earn money and make your way in the world, unencumbered by debt, will be a great feeling.

But, as with all things in life, pay attention and proceed thoughtfully. Sadly, there are people out there who may not have your best interests at heart. Do your research and trust your instincts.

The 21st century is turning out to be exciting and unpredictable. The labour market is changing fast and it is an exciting time to be entering a new career – but it is also daunting. My sense is that, having got all the way through this book, you are going to be well set up to find an apprenticeship and convert that into a great career.

As with all things in life, remember to listen to good advice but do not forget to back yourself.

I hope you enjoy whatever it is you end up doing!

### APPRENTICE CASE STUDY: MICHAELA CLACK

Wouldn't it be amazing to be able to ask someone who did both an apprenticeship and a university degree before they started their career what they thought?

Fortunately, we can.

Michaela is an Account Director at global affiliate marketing business, Awin Global. Working her way up rapidly from entry level she is now an Account Director managing 25 people – and she still has a few years to go before she turns 30. Her clients include the likes of Virgin Media, Samsung and O2/Giff Gaff. She has been able to live and work in Barcelona, and is now enjoying the fact that the firm runs a four-day week (for full pay!).

'I left school with uninspiring A level results – because I was uninspired by academic work – and found my calling at a startup media company called Contentive – based in the building on the other side of the road from my school.'

At the startup, Michaela did a 12-month apprenticeship in social media: 'My apprenticeship changed and shaped my life.' For Michaela, the combination of real work experience woven into the qualification itself was powerful.

However, she still felt she was missing something, so used her apprenticeship to get into one of the very first Digital Marketing degrees, at the University of Portsmouth.

When Michaela is asked which was more important for securing her first role with Awin, her apprenticeship or her degree, there is no hesitation: 'My apprenticeship, by far. It enabled me to learn what it was like to operate in a workplace – initially quite intimidating by the way! But it gave me so much confidence.' She also notes how powerful it is to have the blend of real work experience with a qualification.

She really enjoyed university too, a time during which, by living away from home, she learned valuable life skills and made some great friends. But from a career point of view, it was the apprenticeship that had the biggest impact.

As a senior manager and responsible for hiring new people herself, she does not look at where the person went to university, still less what grade they got (which is different from what her school told her employers would do). What Michaela wants to see when she assesses someone for a job is their work experience and track record – what has the person actually done? What have they achieved?

'It was these questions that made the difference at my first interview – and my answers all came from my time as an apprentice, not from my course at university.'

## EMPLOYER CASE STUDY: MBDA

MBDA is a unique multi-national European group, a world-leader in the field of complex weapon systems playing a key role in keeping nations safe. The company generates over €14billion per year in revenue and employs over 14,000 people across Europe and the USA.

In the UK, MBDA recruits around 50 apprentices every year, and as the company's business continues to grow they expect this number to rise further.

'Our Early Careers programmes in the UK are a key part of our talent strategy, and apprenticeships are a key part of this,' says Andrew Marchant, the Early Careers Programmes Lead for MBDA UK. 'Our next intake in September 2023 will bring our total number of apprentices to around 150.' The company also hires a large number of graduates – totalling around 280 on their graduate schemes by the autumn of 2023 – meaning that around 8% of their UK workforce will be either an apprentice or a graduate.

MBDA UK apprenticeships cover a wide range of roles in the company. There are many covering the different aspects of engineering, such as mechanical, electrical, systems and, more recently, software engineering. As MBDA UK and, in turn, their apprenticeship schemes have grown and developed, there are now even more apprentice roles on offer in the operational side of the company, such as sales, procurement, finance, commercial and information management.

The championing and support for apprenticeships comes from the very top at MBDA UK. There are many senior leaders in the business that started as apprentices themselves. They appreciate that the right structure, development and support can enable anyone right at the start of their career to be successful in future, perhaps becoming a business leader too.

Apprenticeships, and MBDA UK's other Early Careers programmes, which include undergraduate and summer placements as well as graduate schemes, have delivered measurable business benefits. Andrew says, 'Apprenticeships also help us increase the diversity of our workforce. It's really pleasing to see the wide mix of people across genders, ethnicities and the neurodivergent. We're keen to make sure we are open and accessible to all, and our intakes increasingly reflect this aspiration.' A diverse workforce also brings a diversity of thought, and Andrew adds, 'We are in the business of innovation at MBDA. Having people with different backgrounds, experiences and ways of thinking maximises our chances of seeing different possibilities and having a successful, innovative company. It also makes us a very nice place to work!'

Andrew goes on to explain how apprenticeships work at MBDA, typically occurring over a four-year period. 'Apprentices are doing real work, in a team, alongside experienced colleagues who they learn from on-the-job and wider apprenticeship programme activities,' he says. 'They then have off-the-job study at a local college or university, learning the theory behind what they are doing or will do in the future. It's also an opportunity to benchmark themselves against apprentices from other companies. End Point Assessment then gives a rigorous and objective validation of everything they have done.'

Apprenticeships, Andrew says, are for those who want to move beyond just academic study, to start their working life and who want to grow and still achieve their qualifications to support their future career.

On the decision about whether to do an apprenticeship, Andrew has some useful (and familiar) advice: 'First, don't put yourself under pressure that this is a one-off decision – it's not. If something doesn't work out, you have other options. A career is a marathon not a sprint.'

On career paths, Andrew has further advice, saying, 'Career paths are often not a straight line. They can be a rather wiggly line for some at times. It's all about personal choice. It doesn't have to be about vertical progression. For those that want to try different things it can be far more diverse (or wiggly). It depends on what you want to achieve and the skill sets you want or need to develop.'

Due to the growth in the number of apprenticeships on offer in the UK, MBDA is aware that potential apprentices could find the choice of apprenticeship difficult. Andrew offers some things to think about in this regard: 'When figuring out whether an employer might be good for your apprenticeship, try to work out how important apprenticeships are for them. When you meet people at the company, how friendly and open are they? Do they welcome challenging questions or try to shut them down? Can they explain the role apprenticeships play in their company? Do they have examples of success? The more open they are, the more they explain the role apprentices play in the business, the more likely the programme is strong and will better aid an apprentice's development and their future career.'

Andrew adds that in addition to looking at ratings on websites such as ratemyapprenticeship.co.uk and OFSTED results for ideas as to where to study, applicants should also read the reviews carefully and look at the apprenticeship awards businesses have won.

The final piece of advice Andrew offers for any aspiring apprentice successful in getting on a scheme is: 'Take advantage of everything on offer. Obtain clarity about how you can thrive and develop, and do not be afraid to ask for support and help. Never be afraid to ask questions!'

# Section 10
# Useful resources

Here are the various websites and other resources mentioned throughout the guidebook, all in one place:

General careers websites:

- nationalcareers.service.gov.uk
- prospects.ac.uk

The official list of available Apprenticeship Standards:

- instituteforapprenticeships.org/apprenticeship-standards

There are good case studies here:

- engage.apprenticeships.gov.uk/aan-testimonials

Websites with information, guidance and live apprenticeship opportunities:

- amazingapprenticeships.com
- notgoingtouni.co.uk
- apprenticeshipguide.co.uk
- allaboutschoolleavers.co.uk
- careermap.co.uk

To check out specific universities and courses:

- officeforstudents.org.uk

To check out specific employers:

- glassdoor.co.uk

To check out specific training providers:

- reports.ofsted.gov.uk

To get advice and guidance if you have a disability:

- Disability Rights UK student hotline: **0330 995 0414** (free), or **students@disabilityrightsuk.org**.

Links for the Disabled Apprentice Network:

- disabilityrightsuk.org/disabled-apprentice-network
- pathwaygroup.co.uk/disabled-apprentice-network

For Government support for people with disabilities or who are non-typical:

- gov.uk/access-to-work
- ablefutures.org
- neurodiversityinbusiness.org
- digitaladvantage.org.uk
- mind.org.uk has some useful information, e.g. around the application process mind.org.uk/information-support/legal-rights/discrimination-at-work/telling-my-employer

Links to the Multicultural Apprenticeship Alliance:

- linkedin.com/company/multiculturalaa/?originalSubdomain=uk (Join LinkedIn to access this)
- pathwaygroup.co.uk/multiculturalaa

For advice and guidance once you have become an apprentice:

- associationofapprentices.org.uk

To understand your full take home pay after:

- moneysavingexpert.com/tax-calculator

To apply for an apprenticeship (this list is not exhaustive! Search online to get even more possibilities):

- gov.uk/apply-apprenticeship (England)
- careerswales.gov.wales/apprenticeship-search (Wales)
- apprenticeships.scot (Scotland)
- nidirect.gov.uk/services/search-apprenticeship-opportunities (Northern Ireland)
- ucas.com
- amazingapprenticeships.com
- getmyfirstjob.co.uk
- allaboutcareers.com
- notgoingtouni.co.uk
- apprenticeshipguide.co.uk
- allaboutschoolleavers.co.uk
- careermap.co.uk
- reed.co.uk/apprenticeships

Information on other government-funded non-apprenticeship programmes:

- Supported internships: **gov.uk/government/publications/supported-internships-for-young-people-with-learning-difficulties/supported-internships**
- Bootcamps: **gov.uk/guidance/find-a-skills-bootcamp**